S0-ARV-567

Empathy Deficit Disorder
Healing from Our Mix-Ups about Work, Home, and Sex

Editor: Elizabeth Brown
Proofreader: Liberty Britz
Indexer: Sandi Schroeder
Art Direction & Book Design: Jeffrey Bauer
Cover Design & Illustration: James Steinberg
Layout & Graphic Production: Giraffe, Inc.

For information about special discounts for bulk purchases,
please contact Acho & Basilion sales at jacho@theachogroup.com.

$12.95
ISBN 978-1-7324364-0-4
51295>

9 781732 436404

Printed and bound in the United States of America

www.empathydeficitdisorder.com

Empathy Deficit Disorder

Healing from
Our Mix-Ups about
Work, Home, and Sex

Authored • Published by
Jacqueline Acho, PhD, & Eva Basilion, MS

To our Parents
And all people who do their best to nourish empathy in children

To our Husbands
And all the men who lean into the power of empathy

To our Children
With your generation, the world is in good hands

CONTENTS

The Future Can Be Empathic ... and #Sexy

Appendices

Back

Signs of Our Empathy Deficit Disorder

E mpathy is the greatest of all human powers. It is the glue of humanity. It is how humans connect with each other to create something bigger and better than any one person can do alone. Empathy is responsible for our biological existence as well as our ability to make our way in the world. Without it, we could not flourish. We could not survive. We could not evolve. We could not exist.

In this rapidly changing world, empathy is being increasingly recognized as the resource that will fuel our economy and our way of life moving forward. Unfortunately, this resource seems to be compromised today. Our country is suffering from an empathy deficit, and it is causing a lot of pain. Do you see it? Do you feel it? If not, this book is not for you. Not right now anyway.

We see the signs of our empathy deficit disorder everywhere. Our babies are dying at rates that rival the infant mortality statistics of far poorer nations, despite the fact that we spend more on health care than anyone else. Although we hyperparent and focus on schools, our children are experiencing an unprecedented rise in anxiety and depression.

Things are looking dismal at work too. Most people—70%, or ~70 million people—say they are not engaged at work.[1] Not engaged during most of their waking hours. Every day, it seems another one of our bosses is being indicted for a serious crime, including rape, mass environmental poisoning, or the manipulation of our private data. And still today, leadership remains largely white and male. Over 50 years after the feminist revolution, women are not leading.

It's not just women. Our penal system is shooting and incarcerating our Black men at disproportionate rates. And it's not just our Black men. Even white men, the demographic most prevalent in leadership, are dying, too often by their own hand, whether holding a drink, a needle, or a gun. White men in the US are the first demographic in all of world history to have *increasing* mortality—here, now, in one of the richest countries on earth at a time of so much progress. It's puzzling. Sometimes men take us with them in mass shootings that end in suicide. It seems we are collateral damage in a kind of self-loathing we do not yet understand. Every massacre still catches us off guard.

No matter which side of the climate change debate you believe, the unprecedented rise in environmental toxicity and increasing natural disasters show a gaping lack of empathy for future generations and, many would say, for the earth itself. A sense of foreboding about the future is apparently not lost on Millennials, either. They are voting with their reproductive organs, opting not to have children, putting the US fertility rate at an all-time low.[2] There is more than one way for this all to end. The world is not all doom and gloom, of course, but the fist step in solving a problem is admitting you have one. Any one of these issues should have our attention. Altogether, they are a wake-up call none of us should sleep through.

How did we get here?

This empathy deficit disorder is the result of an economic system built on the separation of work and home. This separation has devalued the most foundational form of empathy—the emotional, embodied, so-called affective empathy that is our birthright. As a result, we have forgotten who we are.

The separation of work and home is something we have long taken for granted as necessary for economic viability. It is a narrative so deeply embedded in our collective psyche that we have accepted it as truth. But is it still necessary?

In this book, we will look at this question by examining long-held assumptions upon which this separation was founded. We will revisit these assumptions, or "mix-ups," about what leadership is, what children need, and what it means to be a man or woman in today's world. And we will ask: Do we still believe these things? Do they still serve us in some way? If not, what is it that we do believe today? And how should these beliefs shape our path moving forward?

Like any of the stories we tell ourselves about how the world works and our place in it, these myths can evolve as we learn. An alternative paradigm based on co-creation is presented as a new way forward—a new way that grows rather than depletes our empathy. It is possible now in ways that were economically unviable before. By aligning our new external reality with our innermost humanity, co-creation offers a solution to our empathy deficit disorder and an opportunity to unite our divided world.

Empathy is *that* powerful.

*

CHAPTER 1

The Human
Power of Empathy

What is empathy? Empathy is the ability to feel and understand the inner emotional experience of another, as if it were one's own. It was translated from the German word *Einfühlung*, meaning "infeeling" or "feeling into," coined in philosopher Robert Vischer's PhD thesis in 1873.[3]

Empathy is a word we use to represent a complex soup of cognitive, emotional, and physical responses that are a unique part of the human experience. Many different fields have their take on empathy—neuroscience, cognitive psychology, evolutionary biology, sociology, economics, and so on. It can be confusing. There are many different facets to this gem of empathy, and we will look at several of them.

Empathy is generally differentiated into two major components: *Cognitive* Empathy and *Affective* Empathy.

Cognitive Empathy:	A thinking activity. It occurs in conscious awareness. It is the ability to identify and understand another's feelings. Sometimes we call this kind of empathy "perspective taking." Cognitive empathy allows me to know what you are feeling. But it doesn't mean that I have to share that feeling.

Affective Empathy: A feeling activity. It is also called emotional empathy or primitive empathy. It is unconscious and happens automatically, outside of our awareness. It is the ability to share another's emotions. Affective empathy allows me to feel what you are feeling. We feel it in our bodies before we even recognize it as an emotion.

THE ORIGINS OF EMPATHY

Where does our capacity for empathy come from? Few people have studied this topic more than Professor Frans de Waal of Emory University. He wrote a brilliant book called *The Age of Empathy*, in which he summarizes the latest research, including his own work with primates. De Waal tells us that not only are we born with empathic capacity, but it's also been in our human family for a long time. The capacity for affective empathy came with the evolution of the limbic system—the feeling brain.[4]

Underlying this earliest capacity is specialized brain activity, something researchers are just starting to understand. Mammals with mirror self-recognition (the ability to recognize one's image in a mirror) also possess a rare and specialized type of brain cell called VEN cells (a.k.a. Von Economo neurons). These cells are found in abundance in the anterior insular cortex of our brains, the part that controls behaviors we consider to be human.

But this is just the beginning. Empathy is more than simple mirroring or emotional contagion. Once the tracks for affective empathy are laid down, our capacity for cognitive empathy emerges. According to de Waal, "The full capacity [for empathy] seems put together like a Russian doll. At its core is an automated process shared with a multitude of species, surrounded by outer layers that fine-tune its aim and reach."[5]

Empathy as a whole is a complex skill involving many areas of our brains and bodies. Few people have a better handle on the neuroscience of empathy than Cambridge University professor Simon Baron-Cohen, author of *The Science of Evil: On Empathy and the Origins of Cruelty*. Baron-Cohen says that there are at least ten interconnected brain regions involved in empathy. For these complex reactions, several areas of the brain appear to form an empathy circuit. Each region of the brain contributes something— from the medial prefrontal cortex (MPFC) in self-awareness, to the amygdala, which is important for emotional learning and self-regulation.[6]

AFFECTIVE EMPATHY IS A CONTACT SPORT

As we have seen, affective empathy develops first and lays the foundation for cognitive empathy. It starts in our bodies, the day we are born or even in utero. It develops before we have words, back when we communicated with bodily feeling states. Remember that? You probably don't have cognitive memories, but according to child development experts, people do have

7

"feeling memories" of the time before words. Everyone who was ever an infant has experience with bodily empathy. This means YOU.

Feeling sleepy? So do we. Did you know picking up yawns is a reflection of empathy? It's one of the most primitive forms of embodied empathy. Affective empathy is part of the two-way communication between infant and parent. It is the means by which a baby's physical needs are met. When you were hungry, you fussed or cried. Mom or dad sensed your hunger and were moved to respond by feeding you. You took in the feeding and felt satisfied. Until the next time.

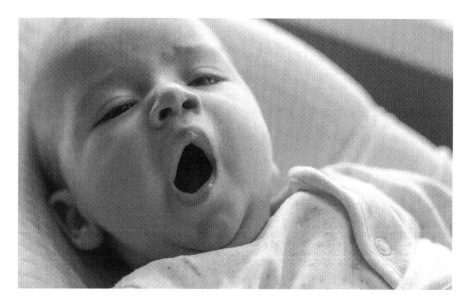

But affective empathy does more than just satisfy physical needs. It's a two-way dance between parent and infant that meets the profound human need for recognition. The baby learns that he exists because his parent exists. Through gaze, smell, touch, taste, and sound, the parent and infant become unconsciously attuned to each other. A trust in the relationship develops, *setting the template for future relationships.* Attunement provides the model for affective empathy that the child carries with him throughout life.

If you were one of the unlucky ones, sometimes mom or dad was nowhere to be found—physically and perhaps even emotionally. This can happen when a mother suffers from postpartum depression, for example. When the dance of attunement is interrupted, the child does not receive validation of his feelings, and he may fail to thrive. It is a situation all too common in orphanages around the world. Sometimes the baby dies.

Despite the fact that affective empathy is a life-giving force, it is often the forgotten stepsister of what we think about when we use the word empathy—which is the cognitive type. Some scientific fields omit affective empathy altogether from working definitions of empathy. The unconscious nature of emotions means they are a challenge to quantify with basic scientific tools, requiring special creativity and cross-disciplinary study. Not everyone is up to the task.

Acknowledging affective empathy can also be inconvenient. It can feel like a square peg in the round hole of a system that favors efficiency and devalues caring work—the type of work that develops this kind of empathy. Thanks to better neuroscientific imaging techniques and evolutionary biology's growing interest in the field, however, affective empathy is making a comeback.

COGNITIVE EMPATHY: IT IS SELFISH FIRST

Here is something most people usually don't discuss when it comes to cognitive empathy. It is selfish first. What we mean is that one must know himself before he can relate to others. A concept of selfhood is a prerequisite to mature empathy.

We take for granted our perspective as individuals in a community, but sense of self wasn't always possible, collectively or individually. Over time, the awakening of a sense of self brought our species out of the collective prehistoric fog of our hunter-gatherer forebearers. Individuality continued to grow. Today, sense of self is especially evident in countries such as the US, which exalts it.

On an individual level, it isn't until 18–24 months of age that a child begins to develop a sense of self. Have you ever seen a toddler discover and love on herself in a mirror? What you witnessed was beyond adorable; it was the signal of important and relatively unique brain development called mentalization. When a child reaches mentalization, she is able to recognize another person's mind as different from her own, consciously understanding that thoughts and feelings underlie behavior. It is at this point that children have the capacity to develop cognitive empathy, the ability to imagine another perspective. Empathy becomes represented in thoughts.

Once the capacity for cognitive empathy emerges, empathy development becomes conscious and more deliberate, utilizing a new set of tools. While empathy continues to be shaped by its affective foundation, now forces based in language and ideas begin to make their mark. Education is one such tool. The use of rewards and punishment, such as praise or shame, is another. All of these cognitive tools are at their best when the cognitive continues to work with the affective. When the cognitive (imagining abstractly how another person feels) becomes disconnected from the affective (actually feeling tangibly in our bodies the way another person feels), problems ensue.

Another way of understanding the connection between affective and cognitive empathy is through the concept of "conscience." What people generally refer to as "conscience" can be a mediator between our affective state (how we feel), our cognition (how we think about how we feel), and our behavior (what we do about it). When we think or do something that contradicts our affective empathy template, we may feel pain in the form of cognitive dissonance (a feeling that does not follow the story we tell ourselves). This dissonance signals us to reassess our thoughts and behaviors with the chance of making things "right." In this sense, "right" means a realignment of our affective and cognitive states. "Right" can also mean "moral." When this mediator is no longer working properly, our thoughts and actions fail to be properly informed.

WHEN THINGS GO WRONG

Affective and cognitive empathy need each other. Though one is based in the realm of emotion and the other in the realm of cognition, the potential of each is maximized when they remain in constant conversation. Our complex and interconnected brains are built for this conversation. But sometimes the line of communication is broken. And that's when things go wrong.

Psychiatrists have recognized several psychiatric illnesses associated with an empathy deficit. According to Baron-Cohen, sociopathy, narcissism, and borderline personality disorders are defined by a diminished capacity for empathy. De Waal takes it a step further and says that psychopaths suffer from a permanent disconnect between perspective taking (considering how another person feels) and the deeper regions of emotional empathy (actually feeling it). In this diagnosis, he includes both serial killers and CEOs.[7] In other words, some people feel like the empty shell of the Russian doll of empathy.

In such cases, cognitive empathy may be completely intact, if not stronger than usual. But without its older sister of affective empathy weighing in, cognitive empathy can be a tool of manipulation. A sociopath knows full well the pain he is causing you—he just enjoys it. Without the affective empathy weighing in, the other person is erased, showing up as projection rather than a real person. It becomes easy to overlook their feelings and reactions and simply satisfy his own. Think of the abuser who believes he has a right to a woman's body without her consent.

But this dysfunction has another face. It also looks like fusion—becoming so fused with another that individual identities are lost. Fusion can look so empathic on the surface. Think of the mother who spoils her child because she projects her own feelings and emotions of pain, loss, fear, hope, etc. onto the child. Think of the lover who becomes a victim of physical abuse and stays because she has forgotten that she counts, too. Patriarchy is not empathy. But neither is matriarchy.

Affective empathy without an appropriate level of cognitive empathy presents its own problems. Autism spectrum disorders are said to fit this profile.[8] In this case, people can experience emotional overload in the presence of others, because the complexity of human behaviors and relationships is overwhelming in the midst of the feelings they are taking in. This makes it difficult to function in society as we know it.

Scientists are still trying to understand what goes wrong when empathy function is compromised. Are functions eliminated, or is it that communication between the cognitive and affective becomes compromised? Do some people have a more fluid dialogue between these two areas of the brain, while in others they are more compartmentalized? We're only just starting to understand how all of this works. It's awesome, really— what our brains are figuring out about our brains. Keep your eyes on this research. There is more to come.

"Mirror neurons promise to do for neuroscience what DNA did for biology," says neurobiologist V. S. Ramachandran of the University of California, San Diego, in a 2005 Wall Street Journal article. To him, this explains "a host of mental abilities that have remained mysterious."[9]

Even the Wall Street Journal has been paying attention to empathy for a while now. Shouldn't we?

CAN EMPATHY BE BAD?

Some people think so. The latest research is exciting, but the modern scientific tendency toward reductionism can be misleading. Take, for example, cognitive psychologist Paul Bloom in his book *Against Empathy* As Baron-Cohen points out, "For Bloom, empathy only occurs when you have the identical or mirror emotion to another person. 'If you feel bad for someone who is bored, that's sympathy, but if you feel bored, that's empathy,' Bloom writes."[10] Bloom's empathy sounds a lot like fusion, doesn't it? It's also incomplete. Baron-Cohen continues, "In contrast, I and most other empathy theorists use a much broader definition of empathy: Empathy is having an appropriate emotion triggered by another person's emotion."[11] That sounds more like affective and cognitive empathy working together in a co-creative way between two people.

A relatively new but clarifying voice in empathy research is Jamil Zaki, assistant professor of psychology at Stanford, and the director of the Stanford Social Neuroscience Laboratory. He also thinks Bloom has reduced empathy too far. He says:

> *Scientists can differentiate between these "pieces" of empathy, for instance, because they activate different systems in the brain. But just because two things can be separated doesn't mean they are always or even usually neatly divided. People can tell the difference between chickpeas and olive oil, but real world empathy is more like hummus—blended, often for the better.[12]*

Yes. Hummus. One part affective. One part cognitive. Stir well.

Our scientific understanding of this human power of empathy will continue to evolve, hopefully in ever more wise, holistic, and mature ways. When the wisest grandmothers and yogis start nodding their heads at the emerging findings, we'll know things are moving in the right direction.

BELIEVE IT OR NOT, EMPATHY IS RISING

Despite our lack of understanding and various cultural hurdles, over the long arc of time, empathy is rising. Jeremy Rifkin plumbs the history of empathy development, setting up an intriguing dichotomy between the physical and emotional worlds. "At the very core of the human story is the paradoxical relationship between empathy and entropy."[13]

Rifkin sees two driving forces:

1. empathy, which is unlimited, and
2. entropy (the disorder resulting from energy consumption), which is limited, ultimately by the sun.

Both of these forces have fueled global development from the beginning of time. For most of history, mankind has put them at odds; but it is theoretically possible for entropy and empathy to increase together. This may have been true in civilizations that lived in greater harmony with the earth and each other. And we might learn more from these models if we had not written them so blithely out of the popular history books. Native Americans. Pre-colonial matriarchal Africa.[14] The culture and history experts tell us they lived in ways that felt more abundant. And abundance changes everything.

But so much about modern culture is not rooted in abundance. European man climbing out of caves at the end of the Ice Age had no such luxury. Scarcity was real. The earth, a harsh place. Competition, on! And so it went for many generations until today, with increasing consumption and competition, in the midst of real and perceived physical scarcity. To what end? A good one, in many ways.

There is a lot to celebrate in today's standard of living. The data point to better lives for most people on earth, increased global connectivity, as well as the possibility of abundance for everyone—with *no new technology*.[15]

Such are the benefits of industrial processes, which have been making things better, cheaper, and faster, giving rise to the network and resulting in decreasing marginal costs.

But there have been entropic costs to amassing and expending energy in all of its forms (e.g., food, fossil fuels, firepower). We manifest in the world that to which we attend. If we're busy competing for food or energy reserves, empathy will be on the proverbial back burner. This low priority for empathy is especially true in times of real and perceived scarcity when competition for resources gets intense; getting enough requires all of our attention. Sometimes, it requires a fight too. Empathy is in many ways the opposite of competition.

Still, despite the highly profitable, fear-inducing images of 24/7 media these days, Rifkin makes a compelling case that the human capacity for empathy has been generally rising from the beginning of time until now. He's not the only one helping us cut through the hype. Yuval Harari, in his historical take on our species, *Sapiens: A Brief History of Humankind*, lays out some intriguing and relevant facts too. "Out of the 57 million dead [in 2002], only 172,000 died in war and 569,000 died of violent crime (a total of 741,000 victims of human violence)."[16] That's just 1.3%. Ironically, in that year of 2002, you were more likely to die by your own hand (873,000 suicides) than someone else's. He goes on, "In most parts of the world, people go to sleep without fearing that in the middle of the night a neighboring tribe might surround their village and slaughter everyone." Statistically, the world has gotten less violent over time, even though it doesn't always feel that way.

The implications for ever-rising empathy are big and exciting in Rifkin's view: "empathy becomes the window to the divine. It is by empathic extension that we transcend ourselves and begin connecting with the mystery of existence."[17]

But we still have a long way to go.

WHERE DO WE GO FROM HERE?

Despite the importance of empathy, our current societal systems work against our abilities to practice it. If you try to empathize, it hurts—because the system punishes you. If you try *not* to empathize, it also hurts—because you are denying your most basic human instinct to connect.

But it's not empathy's fault. And it's not our fault either. It's the system. There is no room for empathy. Not yet. Perhaps these systems are no longer serving us. Let's take a look...

Clearing Up Our Mix-Ups about Work, Especially Leadership

CHAPTER 2

Mix-Up No. 1
Leadership Is One Guy at the Top of a Pointy Pyramid

"Freedom is just another word for nothing left to lose…"
—Janis Joplin, "Me and Bobby McGee," 1971

Work isn't working these days. Because we have a mix-up. And it starts at the top. We are mixed up about what leadership is.

Meet the pointy pyramid. What we saw in the grand pyramids of Egypt (built by millions of slaves, by the way) remains reflected today in the organizational structures of the majority of our institutions. Today, we still believe that leadership must be a hierarchy, with one guy at the top of a pointy pyramid. Leaders remain synonymous with positional authority. We simply can't imagine another model.

Yet, increasing evidence suggests that hierarchical models sap affective empathy and reinforce bad behavior—with detrimental consequences for our economy. If that's what leadership looks like today, maybe it's time to rethink what it means to truly lead. It seems we are mixed up about what leadership is.

Leadership is commonly defined as "the art of motivating people to act towards achieving a common goal."[18] This is what leadership looks like in reality.

Leadership as usual is an **individual sport.** It's a solo dance with one guy on the hook at the top of a pyramid. It's a **monologue,** a one-way conversation (or even just a tweet) from top to bottom. How many CEOs do you know who are great listeners? The pyramid attracts **workaholics,** because face time and billable hours are rewarded. It's honey to busy bees who enjoy working for a host of healthy and less healthy (i.e., addiction) reasons.

And the job is egregiously **compensated.** The definition of compensation is so telling: "Something, typically money, awarded to someone as a recompense for loss, injury, or suffering."[19] That's right. Do you remember how much Oracle CEO Larry Ellison earned at the end of his tenure? $96.2 million a year. Let's do the math. Assuming he worked 100 hours a week, 52 weeks a year, that works out to $18,500/hour—all the while his board and the analysts applauded. What could he possibly have been *doing* in that hour?

Even though shared leadership structures such as co-CEOs and innovative partnerships are becoming more common, most boards can't fathom new models. Rather than encouraging partnership, boards seem to prefer a workplace version of the reality TV show *Survivor*—where survival of the fittest and competition reign supreme. We may believe in democracy, especially in the US, but our organizations don't actually practice it. We put leaders on a pedestal and believe (or pretend, or hope) that they have all the answers, when we know the real answers include everyone. We isolate leaders at the top of the pyramid, with the pointy end of that triangle sticking straight up their...

It's not comfortable. It's not even humane. Isolation is the harshest form of punishment we can inflict on our fellow human beings; at least in solitary confinement, you don't have to guess who is telling you the truth or not. It really is **lonely** at the top. It's no wonder leaders are so often cranky.

The problem is that we have all bought into this mix-up. We shouldn't comfort ourselves with the idea that leaders are different from the rest of us. We are all complicit. We hate mansplaining[20]—when people talk down to us in a patronizing manner (or as Rebecca Solnit put it, *Men Explain Things to Me*[21])—but isn't that what we ask leaders to do? We take comfort in having one guy at the top; it helps us sleep at night. All of us—employees, boards, investors, voters—find relief in knowing there is a mantle where we can lay our troubles. Or at least lay our blame and shame. We may have a sinking feeling about the future, but at least it's not on us, right? We transfer authority, rather than share responsibility. Unfortunately, this transfer has made leadership impossible.

Many commonly accepted "leadership traits" (dominance, tough-mindedness, self-assurance, compulsiveness, etc.) are simply a euphemistic rebranding of narcissism, or worse. For many people, the realities of leadership have become repulsive. Not something to which they aspire, even as a channel for considerable talent and years of relevant experience. Power may be an aphrodisiac, but the sad irony is that modern leadership is most often not attractive.

HOW DID WE GET HERE?

We redefined human nature as heartless and selfish in a couple of important ways. We disembodied Adam Smith's invisible hand, and we let Herbert Spencer adapt Darwin's evolutionary theories for business. Our economics were rational. Our cash, cold and hard. Our motivation, survival via competition. With these paradigms, we erased empathy from the equation of how we relate to each other in most of our working and waking moments. For 300 years, this idea that human beings are fundamentally selfish has been ingrained.

In hindsight, it is not hard to see how this came to be. If we could convince ourselves that we were fundamentally selfish, then we could apply Darwin's principle of "survival of the fittest" to business to justify the moral dilemmas that emerged during the industrial revolution. Herbert Spencer, an English political theorist and Victorian philosopher, did just that to a willing audience in 1864 with his book *Principles of Biology*. Social Darwinism is still invoked to this day by politicians, business leaders, and quite memorably by Michael Douglas as Gordon Gekko in the movie *Wall Street*. Wearing slicked-back hair and suspenders while invoking the "evolutionary spirit," he crooned, "Greed is good!"[22] Ah, the '80s.

Yet empathy is not just a recent phenomenon. As mentioned earlier, it's been with us for a very long time, since we evolved our limbic system, home of the feeling brain. Evolutionary biologists are showing we could never have survived as a species with competition alone. According to de Waal, empathy is the "glue that holds entire societies together."[23] It turns out that empathy has been an equal, if not more powerful, driver of our evolution.

Empathy is necessary because each of us is different; empathy is possible because we are the same. It's really that simple. Remaining selfish is a choice, not an incontrovertible scientific fact. It may be the most convenient choice for a time, but in the end, it's a dangerous choice. Because no man can remain an island, unless he wishes to eventually self-destruct. Empathy is the antidote, a superpower of proportions we are only now beginning to imagine.

CHAPTER 3

The Corporate
Psychopath

L et's go back to our definition of leadership: "The art of motivating
people to act towards a common goal." In hierarchical structures, it is
not clear that anyone is really being motivated by anything other than fear.
And it is not clear that common goals are being achieved, since authentic
conversations are infrequent. The way we have conceived of leadership is
failing to meet our most fundamental goals—and worse. In addition, our
systems are doing harm. By facilitating an environment absent of affective
empathy, our systems repel the men and women who would make the best
leaders. So, who rises? Meet the corporate psychopath.

For a classic example of a psychopath, think of Anthony Hopkins as the
movie character Hannibal Lecter—the steely-eyed serial killer. Charming,
self-confident, and cultured. But mean, to say the least. Manipulative,
sadistic, unable to feel remorse. Prefers fava beans and Chianti…to go
with his victim's liver. Sounds disgusting. But what about in corporations?
Do psychopaths exist in the C-suite? You betcha. It's not everyone, of
course, but we bet you know someone who has these tendencies, because…

While psychopaths represent 1% of the general population, a 2010 study suggests that they make up at least 4% of managerial positions in corporations.[24]

And it's only getting worse.[25] According to a more recent study, the rate of psychopaths in the upper echelons of corporations is as high as 20%, the same prevalence of psychopaths found in the prison population.

We have seen them in the headlines for a long time, and there is no sign of that news slowing down:

- Bernie Madoff (such an ironic name) who went to jail for stealing money from clients in the largest financial fraud in US history.[26] People were fascinated by his unprecedented Ponzi scheme. Sounds like the plot of a made-for-TV movie? It was, after the fact. You can't make this stuff up.

- Chainsaw Al Dunlap chopped heads gleefully at Sunbeam until it was so broken they had no choice but to file for bankruptcy in 2001.[27] The irony there is that the analysts applauded, until they didn't.

- Roger Ailes resigned from Fox News in 2016 amidst allegations of sexual misconduct.[28] His reward? He became an advisor to then-candidate for US president, Donald Trump, in which capacity he helped with debate preparation. We bet he was really good at it.

- Women are not immune, even where children are concerned. Zero empathy in the corporate world was also in full view recently when CEO Heather Bresch took advantage of Mylan's monopoly and increased the price of the EpiPen by 400%. While putting the life-saving device out of reach for some of the people who needed it most, her total compensation increased from $2.5 million to $19 million.[29]

It's not just people who are bad actors. Corporations are collections of people, sometimes behaving badly. Large organizations too often make decisions as if lives don't matter now, and certainly not in the future. Examples pop up daily. Here are some recent gems:

- After more than a decade of hemming and hawing internally, General Motors (GM) publicly admitted faulty engineering in the ignition switch of millions of their cars.[30] "Sorry" and some money were cold comfort for the 124 families who lost loved ones in the meantime. It wasn't the first time the auto industry sacrificed passenger safety for profit. There was the spectacularly fiery mess of the rear engine Ford Pinto throughout the 1970s.[31] And it won't be the last time, unfortunately.

- Volkswagen's "diesel dupe" was called out by the US Environmental Protection Agency when they realized the company had intentionally fitted the cars with a defeat device that would detect and cheat emissions tests. Engineers can be so clever, and so wrong when they leave their conscience behind.

- Facebook and Cambridge Analytica duped us, too, with clever psychometrics.[32] We're only beginning to understand how much and to what end. What we know is they have our personal data, which has been used without our consent to influence us in the 2016 US presidential election. Time will tell what impact that has.

- Nike executives are being forced out for inappropriate workplace behavior.[33] "Just Do It" may have worked well as a marketing tagline, but as a corporate culture, not so much. Culture can make ordinary people break bad.

And then there is the financial crisis of 2008. You don't have to look far to note that psychopathy was a contributing factor there. Dick Fuld, who was responsible for the demise of Lehman Brothers, was quoted as famously saying, "What I really want to do is I want to reach in, rip out their hearts and eat it before they die."[34]

May we suggest some Chianti with that?

So, what gives?

PSYCHOPATHY AND ITS IMPACT AT WORK

Neuroscience professor Simon Baron-Cohen reminds us that depriving people of empathic development can have a profound effect on personality development and how people relate to others. His research shows us that severe empathy deficits result in behavioral traits we associate with narcissists and psychopaths.

In his book *The Science of Evil*, Baron-Cohen explains that psychopaths are special. They are not completely devoid of empathic skills. In fact, their *cognitive* empathy is often excellent. They know very well how you feel. They can predict and manipulate your behavior. They understand your pain. It's just that they get off on it. When you feel pain, they feel pleasure. Psychopaths are more than immune to the hurt they cause; they enjoy it, or at least find it entertaining. That's not a collapse of cognitive empathy, but rather of affective empathy.

Primatologist Frans de Waal describes psychopathy as a permanent disconnect between taking the perspective of another and the deeper regions of emotional empathy. In other words, the cognitive and affective are no longer communicating. You may remember that affective empathy is the unconscious emotional contagion that is developed body to body between parents and children during the earliest years. That's the piece that stops healthy people from hurting others—because it hurts them, too.

Unless you're a psychopath.

Psychopathy may not affect so many people when it's a bully in a schoolyard. When the bully grows up and gets bigger and stronger, though, collateral damage from bad behavior grows. And sometimes...well, unfortunately as much as 16% of the time according to recent studies...these behaviors make it all the way to the corner office, where they are estimated to be three times more prevalent.[35] The results can be devastating.

Studies show that corporate psychopaths create toxic work environments that lead to conflict, low worker morale, and poor performance. Corporate psychopaths promote conflict by pitting people against each other and bullying subordinates. They neglect their managerial and leadership responsibilities, take credit for the work and ideas of others, and blame others for their own mistakes.[36] Sound familiar? In the news, if not personally?

The internal damage is quick to reflect on the outside. When psychopaths lead organizations, these organizations are less committed to social and environmental responsibility or to the local community. The psychopath's proclivity for risk-taking and fraudulent behavior often costs the organization or even threatens its very existence.[37]

Corporations are logical breeding grounds for psychopathic leadership. For one, psychopathic personalities are motivated by the power and money that are part of corporate leadership, more today than at any other time in our history. Without a conscience to inform their actions, psychopaths operate as purely rational actors, well suited for the rational economic model upon which corporations are based. Without healthy affective empathy, they are also willing to go to great lengths to achieve their goals and do things other people would find unpalatable. Their charm and keen ability to understand the motivations of others allow them to make good impressions and often keep them a step ahead—for a while.

In the process, their affective empathy takes a hit. It's a vicious cycle. And it's not just in corporations, but everywhere we've infused best business practices, especially large organizations. It does not matter whether they are for-profit companies, nonprofit organizations, government, etc. If the pointy pyramid allows psychopathy at the top, what flows down? Not empathy. And the resulting empathy deficit breeds lots of other bad behavior. Why, here comes some more now, and it's not pretty.

MEN BEHAVING BADLY

The egregious sexual harassment and rape allegations against prominent leaders came to a head in the fall of 2017 and threw us all for a loop. Suddenly, some of our most revered leaders were being accused of long-standing patterns of hurting women sexually. It felt shocking, but it shouldn't have. We seek CEOs who are "my way or the highway" types, but then we expect them to sideline this behavior at our convenience. Is that fair? Not really. Which may be why we were all so silent as this behavior took place in front of our eyes. Deep down inside, we are so wed to our vision of leadership that we can't afford to let it go, even to protect ourselves or others who are being violated.

Sometimes we don't even see what's happening as a violation. We accept it as the price of doing business in this system we've all built together. A cost we are willing to pay, personally and collectively. We excuse a US president talking about grabbing women by the p*@sy as "locker room banter." We hear "that's just Harvey being Harvey," as a way to describe from a distance what actually felt at close range like molestation and rape, according to allegations against Harvey Weinstein. We wonder who installed that button under Matt Lauer's desk to lock the door so he could have his way with victims, undisturbed by breaking news or pesky meetings. And how did NBC account for that particular line item, that corner-office perk? A time-saving device for highly paid people who can't be bothered to get up and lock their door...to um, write a memo in privacy? Time is money, after all, especially at $20 million per year.

It is time for a reckoning, all right. It is time for us to question our mix-up about leadership, the one that makes psychopathy the unspoken job description for leaders of our most powerful institutions. We cannot conveniently separate sexual harassment from our leadership mix-up. These are two sides of the same zero-empathy coin.

CORPORATE EMPATHY TRAINING

Organizations are starting to catch on that empathy matters. They are starting to understand the costs of psychopathy and the benefits of empathy to the bottom line. Books have been written and screening tools developed for the purposes of vetting potential employees for psychopathic tendencies. And to ensure that people have enough empathy, empathy training has become all the rage. But is empathy training really the solution? Let's examine.

To make up for the time people don't get at home, we give them "empathy training" at work. If we take the right class from the right teacher, we too can learn empathy, the experts tell us. Organizations are all over it, and empathy training has become a lucrative business. The going rate for a 20-person, 6-session training is $76K.[38]

Sure, education makes a difference. By engaging our rational brains, training helps to bolster the *cognitive* part of empathy. Empathy training can teach us to listen more carefully and better understand the inner emotional workings of the mind. Empathy training helps us find the common human denominators beneath our differences and helps us identify and question our implicit biases.

The problem is that empathy training is a short-term cognitive exercise, layered onto the life experience and emotional health of an individual before and after their time in the classroom. As such, empathy training can only do so much. While cognitive empathy may be improved by empathy school, the affective part of empathy is not so easily accessed in the classroom. Affective empathy is the most primitive, emotional, and automatic part of the empathic response. It's the unconscious part of your reaction. The part that's in your muscle memory, so to speak. Can you *think* your way into six-pack abs? No, you have to *do* the sit-ups. No amount of empathy training at work can match caring for people in real life. We can't so much train affective empathy *into* people as make room for them to practice it.

And what happens when you fortify the cognitive part of empathy without addressing the affective empathy foundation? Ask a psychopath. He'll tell you. Without an underlying working conscience, cognitive empathy becomes a tool for manipulation and personal gain at the expense of others. And that's a problem. It's a problem reflected not just in our leaders but also in the leadership structures in which we house them.

We are starting to see how cruel it is to starve leaders of affective empathy and how that cruelty flows downhill...back to all of us. To society in general. Leadership doesn't feel good these days, not to the leaders or the people being led. We are coming to terms with the psychological costs of separating our leaders from the rest of us. But are these emotional costs the price we must pay for economic viability and success?

Turns out, this style of leadership also falls short when we look at the hard numbers. Hierarchical leadership is not affective. But it's not effective— in economic terms—either. Fewer companies are innovating these days. Leaders do not seem to be spreading the wealth or making the world a better place.

CHAPTER 4

Leadership as Usual
Is Not Effective Because
It Is Not Affective

Clearly, leadership as usual is not working. Whether you lean left and blame business leadership for our issues, or right and blame government leadership for our issues... the common denominator is that we need a different kind of leader.

Having sidelined affective empathy, we have too many psychopaths in power. And we are all suffering the consequences. How do we know? First of all, *no one is following these leaders*. Employees are checked out. Seventy percent of people report they are disengaged at work, according to the most recent Gallup polls.[39] That's 70 million people! They are opting out *emotionally*, if not physically. It's already a *mass migration* upending our economy.

Just a decade after the last crisis, experts are predicting another recession before the year 2020.[40] They say this one could be a real doozy. In the midst of this fear and uncertainty, we search for new policies and blame politicians. Meanwhile, we are the ones who have checked out. Because walking into most organizations makes us hurt.

Millennials are the least engaged of all.[41] Have you noticed? They aren't putting up with the work environments we tolerated. They value time with friends over face time at the office. Not even the best on-site fitness center or bocce court will keep them engaged if the boss is a jerk or their work is exploitive. They are remarkably resistant to the lure of an excellent salary if they feel their work has no soul. For those of us who call Millennials lazy and narcissistic, are we perhaps just envious that they aren't selling out the way many of us did?

Our disengagement is hitting the bottom line. Long-term profitability is hampered by lack of innovation. It's showing up now that there is no more juice in the orange of cost-cutting and outsourcing. Many companies are turning to mergers and acquisitions—M&A—for growth. In fact, M&A is at an all-time high...

> "US companies have proposed or agreed to $627.95 billion worth of mergers or acquisitions this year, the most at this point since Dealogic started tracking figures in 1995."
> —The Wall Street Journal, May 5, 2014

...but M&A continues to destroy rather than create value on average.

> "The sobering reality is that only about 20% of all mergers really succeed. Most mergers typically erode shareholder wealth."
> —M. Grubb and R. Lamb [42]

WHAT HAPPENED TO INNOVATION?

We can still count on organic growth and innovation, right? No. Today, lack of innovation is hurting the profitability of individual companies and our broader economic growth. We're busy beavers with intellectual property piling up.[43] It seems like good news, but are there any really big or productive ideas?

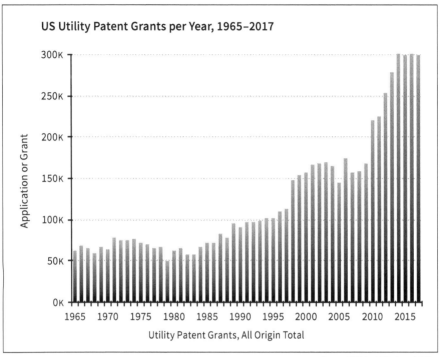

US Utility Patent Grants per Year, 1965–2017

Source: US Patent &Trademark Office

Many people argue there are not. They agree with Buzz Aldrin, astronaut and *Apollo* 11 moonwalker, who lamented to MIT *Technology Review* in 2012, "You Promised Me Mars Colonies. Instead, I Got Facebook."[44] And they have data on their side...

A common measure of innovation, total factor productivity,[45] has been growing at a snail's pace, especially when compared to the glory years of the 1950s, so people wonder if we're out of big ideas.

In addition, studies by the Kauffman Foundation and Brookings Institution using Census Bureau data showed that the number of new companies as a share of all businesses in the US has been dropping for decades, down 44% from 1978 to 2012.[46] Because new businesses have historically been responsible for innovation and economic renewal, economists consider this to be very bad news. Why the decline? Some

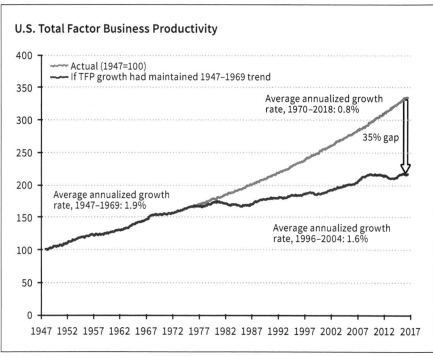

U.S. Total Factor Business Productivity

- Actual (1947=100)
- If TFP growth had maintained 1947–1969 trend

Average annualized growth rate, 1970–2018: 0.8%

35% gap

Average annualized growth rate, 1947–1969: 1.9%

Average annualized growth rate, 1996–2004: 1.6%

Source: Center for the Study of Income and Productivity, Federal Reserve Bank of San Francisco, *The Economist*. From MCK, "Was That It?" *The Economist*, September 8, 2012. Copyright © The Economist Group Limited, London, 2012. Reprinted with permission.

people say Millennials are less risk averse than baby boomers. Experts also point to US population growth shrinking and graying.

Perhaps more importantly, big companies are taking up a lot of the oxygen these days. The expansion of retail, service, and even tech companies squeezes out the competition, e.g., another Panera Bread opening down the street gives the entrepreneurial baker some pause. Furthermore, big companies may not be the launching pads they once were. They have fewer people saddled with more responsibilities, little time for apprenticeship, and seemingly endless cycles of post-merger management from buying little guys to meet innovation goals they could not achieve organically.

Maybe it's getting better? The Kauffman Startup National Activity Index went up slightly in 2016, but new businesses with employees—creating opportunities for more than the founder—are still in a long-term decline since the 1980s. One area that is definitely on the rise—soloists. Since May 2015, 15.5 million people were self-employed in the US, according to the Bureau of Labor Statistics.[47] Intuit predicts soloists will be more than 40% of the US work force by 2020. They are the wildcards. People who can't stomach the big company life. People who hang out a shingle after being downsized, then find life on the outside is better. Parents who want flexibility to work around raising kids. Millennials who want more balance than Google has to offer. People who would rather connect and innovate across virtual and real networks than over cubicle walls, since technology has made the virtual work world boundless. It is not clear how this will all shake out, but we are potentially growing a new ecosystem for innovation which is flatter and more flexible than ever. Time will tell.

IS INNOVATION ALWAYS GOOD?

And what an overused word—*innovation*—right? Not all of it is even good. Great innovation is NOT formulating the next snack chip laced with sugar and MSG that makes us sick and addicted...no matter how much revenues grow. Great innovation is NOT re-purposing old drugs to medicate our children so that they can sit still during school testing. What else? How about the robots that will keep us company in the Alzheimer's unit one day, while our loved ones are busy elsewhere? Maybe they will be on vacation in space by then, since we are making terrific progress on commuter spacecraft—even while one in five children in the US is hungry. As Holly Wood puts it:

> To hear evangelists talk about it, innovation is just awesome science absent any consideration of moral philosophy...These are people who read every scrap of biography of Mark Zuckerberg but have never thought about the terrifying social potential of Facebook's data extraction engine.[48]

Oh no, we can't assume technology will automatically save us. As Matt Ruby on Medium.com puts it:

> *Remember when technology was gonna save us? All these time-saving devices will lead to more efficiency so huzzah, right? And yet everyone is out there relentlessly complaining about how busy they are. Technology didn't save us. It's eating us alive. We don't get any time back, it gets sucked up. Unfettered capitalism doesn't give you time back or freedom or relaxation. It drills every orifice you have until a few more pennies drop out so the Q4 numbers look good for shareholders.* [49]

Certainly not when so much of it is...what it is. Ruby goes on to say:

> *These tech companies position themselves as heroes. They talk about "changing the world" constantly. Yet all they do is churn out technology for rich, white dudes in their 20s/30s who live in big cities and want apps to fill in the blanks for what Mommy used to do.*
> *Mommy used to pick me up from soccer practice. A: Uber.*
> *Mommy used to do my laundry. A: Flycleaners.*
> *Mommy used to clean my room. A: Handy.*
> *Mommy used to buy me groceries. A: Blue Apron.*
> *Mommy used to cook me food. A: Seamless.*
> *And they even call it "mom-tech."* [50]

That's not so bad, but is it good enough? Is it *world-changing* for rich white dudes to have clean shirts, a meal, or a ride so they have more time to work...e.g., to develop the 451st online application for finding the best ramen noodles?

Meanwhile, we're hobbled by inequality. Our political system is undergoing a major disruption. Almost half (43%) of Americans do not trust our judicial system. The climate is warming almost past the point of no return. And one of the wealthiest countries in the world, the United States, also has the highest infant mortality rate in the developed world. We gasp at humanitarian atrocities in other countries, while our own infants are dying.

Are you convinced yet? Positional authority saps affective empathy so much so that it's not helping us emotionally. Positional authority is not helping our economy either. But what is the alternative?

Luckily, the world is changing. It is offering a model for a new type of leadership that makes space for affective empathy. We can look to the future for clues for a new way to be.

CHAPTER 5

The Age of
the Network

The good news is that the world is changing. The industrial revolution is over and the technological revolution is well underway. Advances in the way we communicate continue to alter the world in profound ways, challenging our most basic assumptions about the nature of economics and how we work and live. Some people are excited. Many people are scared.

> "We are witnessing the birth of a new economic system
> that is as different from market capitalism as the
> latter was from the feudal economy of an earlier era."
> —Jeremy Rifkin, Empathic Civilization[51]

The signs of this emerging system are already evident. Music, advice, and education are flooding in for free. 3-D printing is upon us, gearing up to transform and distribute manufacturing to our personal desktops. Publishing will never be the same, now that everyone has a platform and a voice on social media. Who controls the news we consume? Increasingly, our friends on Facebook. The power of health is already in consumers' hands to a greater extent than ever—in health blogs, vegan pins, and meditation apps. Technology is driving something we could have never imagined—nearly free goods and services that are almost priceless to produce. In economic terms, we are approaching the point at which the cost to replicate a good (marginal cost) is zero or near zero. This changes everything.

In his book *Postcapitalism: A Guide to Our Future*, Paul Mason explains: "Until we had shareable information goods, the basic law of economics was that everything is scarce. Supply and demand assumes scarcity. Now certain goods are not scarce, they are abundant—so supply and demand become irrelevant."[52] The irrelevance of supply and demand brings into question the very paradigm upon which capitalism is based.

What does this mean for the future? It's hard to know for sure. Mason believes that we are entering an era of postcapitalism. Rifkin calls it the "Collaborative Commons."[53]

Dov Seidman calls it "The Human Economy."[54] On our way there, our political systems are disrupting, nationalism is rising, terrorism is spreading, and our economy is being dictated by massive monopolies on a scale never before seen. As Joe Brewer puts it plainly in his viral Medium.com post, "That Pain You Feel Is Capitalism Dying."[55] Capitalism as we have come to practice it, anyway. Exactly what it will become next is anyone's guess.

We may not be able to predict the future, but we can better understand what's happening now by asking: What is driving this new economy? As Mason explains, it's not the computer that is responsible for this seismic shift. It's not even the massive amount of information now available to us. The real agent of change is the network—the living, breathing network. He writes: "The network has emerged and has become social."[56]

THE LIVING, BREATHING NETWORK

The global network is alive. It lives and breathes and moves with us. It's all of us, connected across time and space as never before. People not only share information at an unprecedented rate and scale, but we *think* together. We *feel* together. We laugh and cry together. We vent together. We not only share problems and solutions, but we solve together. The network is active like that.

For example, the race is on between the scientist on the hill synthesizing a pill and the migraine or cancer sufferer who is finding kinship and lifesaving nutritional and environmental health advice online. The scale of this knowledge is unprecedented. Search patterns offer huge value, such as finding warning signs for pancreatic cancer before doctors diagnose the disease in patients. The network is smarter than any one doctor can ever be.[57]

We create together, whether on Pinterest or in the blogosphere. We virtually meet people with similar interests, moving each other's projects and ideas forward in real time. We witness together, be it police brutality or championship basketball. We feel collective joy and common outrage. And it's personal. When Lavish Reynolds's boyfriend, 32-year-old Philando Castile, was killed by Minneapolis police, she kept her phone on. She made us look. She made us feel. So did bystanders watching the ambush of police in Dallas a day later.

Joyful waves move through the network too. Euphoria and hometown pride exploded on Facebook, Twitter, and Instagram—across generations and demographics—following the first sports championship in 52 years in Cleveland, Ohio. And the real and virtual worlds collide through people in our lives. We bring new online coworkers, friends, lovers, and even family into our physical midst, while learning new things all the time from what our friends and family choose to post on their Facebook pages.

When Warrensville Heights, Ohio, policewoman and mom Nakia Jones extemporaneously spoke for seven emotional and poignant minutes following the shooting of Black men by police, she relayed her anguish as an officer, a citizen, and a mom. It hit a nerve and was shared more than three million times before the day was done. Migraine or cancer patients can incorporate the best and most possible lifestyle changes to heal and prevent their particular disease, for their particular age, and with the moral support of their family and friends, both real and virtual.

We take all of it in. Then we customize, we individualize, perhaps we contribute through a comment, a post, a share…and then we start all over again, using the connectivity enabled by the network.

We've been told this has been coming for a while. Peter Senge extols the creative power of Synchronicity.[58] Thomas Friedman tells us the world is flat.[59] Whatever you want to call it, connectivity is here. There is no hiding or sticking your head in the sand. The truth will find you. You can no more ignore Beyoncé's next album release than you can forget the images of violence that come flooding into your screen. Now, it really is a small world after all.

THE BEST OF THE NETWORK:
IT'S INCLUSIVE, COLLABORATIVE, SOCIAL, AND RELATIONAL

The network was born back when technology began to make it possible for people to connect at an unprecedented rate and scale. Mason describes the period between 2009 and 2014, and the arrival of the iPhone, streaming video and music, and social media, as the point at which the networked economy coalesced. In the next few years, the Internet of Things will explode as more and more everyday objects acquire the ability to exchange information, extending the network further. Eventually, some people envision that everything and everyone will be connected.[60]

The network is taking on the pointy pyramid in ways we are only just starting to understand. Let us count the ways.

It's Inclusive

The network is inclusive. The more people that are connected, the more value can be created. Kevin Kelly, the first to write about the networked economy, explains this clearly: "Curious things happen when you connect all to all. Mathematicians have proven that the sum of a network increases as the square of the number of members. In other words, as the number of nodes in a network increases arithmetically, the value of the network increases exponentially. Adding a few more members can dramatically increase the value for all members."[61]

In the networked economy, you can't survive playing solo. It's a lot less lonely in that way.

Collaboration Replaces Competition

The network flourishes through the act of collaboration. Collaboration and co-creation replace competition, the cornerstone of market capitalism, calling into question our "survival of the fittest" assumptions about human nature. Rifkin talks about this too:

> Economic activity [is] no longer an adversarial contest between embattled sellers and buyers, but rather a collaborative enterprise between like-minded players. The classical economic idea that another's gain is at the expense of one's own loss is replaced by the idea that enhancing the well-being of others amplifies one's own well-being. The win/lose game gives way to the win/win scenario.[62]

It's Social and Relational

What else? We know that this connectivity is social. Yochai Benkler: "The result is that a good deal more that human beings value can now be done by individuals who interact with each other socially, as human beings and as social beings, rather than as market actors through the price system."[63] That's another way of saying that connectivity is relational. It requires a conversation. Two-way at least.

It Attracts Our Hearts and Minds

Related to the social, it follows that connectivity is not limited to the physical world. It is of the heart and mind. It is internal.[64] Kevin Kelly also saw this coming way back when he wrote, "The only factor becoming scarce in a world of abundance (where everything is free and marginal cost is near zero) is human attention. Each human has an absolute limit of only 24 hours per day to provide attention to the millions of innovations and opportunities thrown up by the economy."[65] Instead of depending on time—time spent "doing," the network depends on attention—on what we are thinking and feeling at a given moment. Workaholism loses its power.

Its Value Is Intrinsic

And finally, the value of the network is intrinsic. When machines do more of our physical and cognitive work, the aim of our labor will be of largely emotional benefit. The rewards will not be external, so monetary compensation has less power. According to Mason, "Non-market forms of production and exchange exploit the basic human tendency … to exchange gifts of intangible value … which has always existed at the margins of economic life."[66]

EMPATHY PROVIDES THE CONNECTIVITY

On what does this living network survive? What does it eat, so to speak? What is this glue that holds people together? What really fuels the win-win we talk so much about but do not as often achieve? This is where empathy comes in.

Rifkin thinks so: "If there is an invisible hand at work, it is that empathy matures.... Empathy becomes the thread that weaves an increasingly differentiated and individualized population into an integrated social tapestry, allowing the social organism to function as a whole."[67]

The connectivity in the network is empathy. It's possible for empathy to be both the motivation and the ultimate outcome of this network, as well as the current that runs through it. The alpha and the omega and everything in between. Perhaps empathy is the fuel on which humanity runs, and the network reflects that—whether the tank is full or empty. Perhaps the network is a mirror of sorts, reflecting us from the inside out. If so, this will be the first time in human history that a living, breathing network moves with us, organizing us at a global scale, rather than a man-made economic or ideological construct or myth acting upon us.

A new leadership model that puts affective empathy at the center may now be possible. It will also be necessary. Because empathy is the fuel of the new economy. It is the very thing that will ensure our success in the future.

CHAPTER 6

Affective Empathy Is
the New Asset Class

*"A new asset class becomes the main basis for productivity
growth, wealth creation, and opportunity. In the agrarian
economy, that asset was land. In the industrial economy, it was
physical capital. In the services economy, it was intangible
assets, such as methods, designs, software, and patents.
In today's knowledge-human economy, it will be human capital—
talent, skills, tacit know-how, empathy, and creativity."*
—Byron August, Co-founder Opportunity@Work, via Thomas Friedman

Let's take this a step further. As the network continues to develop and expand, today's economy is likely to evolve into something less knowledge-based and more human. With machines taking over more of the cognitive work that we do with our heads, cognitive abundance is also becoming a reality. What will remain is the work most essentially human—the work that we do with our hearts. Emotional work. We are moving from "Hands to Heads to Hearts."[68] The networked economy is unveiling an emotional revolution, where value creation relies on empathy, especially emotional empathy.

Empathy is the new asset class. The scarcity that remains will be emotional (fear).

THE ECONOMICS OF EMPATHY

But let's talk about asset classes for a moment. Assets create classes, which is great for some people and bad for others. Winners and losers. Some people seem to be born lucky into the "lucky sperm club." Maybe they inherited a big farm in the 1920s, a profitable manufacturing company in the 1960s, the best education money could buy in the 1990s, or just plain money. A lot of it. To use and invest however they want, no matter how they choose to spend their lives.

For a long time (maybe forever?), we've self-stratified according to whatever is the most valuable asset of our era. Those valuable assets (e.g., land, money, knowledge) afforded some people freedom, power, and opportunity. The more people who could accrue the assets, the more democratic and inclusive a civilization we became. That's why we love meritocracies, because everyone has power to get his share of assets. So, we can live in peace about how well-deserved our own assets are.

The problem is that traditional assets have been anchored in the physical world and so they're inherently limited. Even in the intangible world, limited assets have a compounding effect, because we need assets (like money) to afford assets (like a great education) or any of the other prerequisites to cognitive ability. Prices go through the roof. Some people win and some lose. Inequality grows. Meritocracy doesn't seem so…meritocratic anymore. We thought we left birthrights in ancient history, but wake up to find them still staring at us in the mirror.

Empathy is different. Can you buy it with money? Does it compound with the historical advantages of birth and zip code? Do your excellent education (like a PhD from MIT or master's from Harvard) and corner office job confer the same advantages during the dawning empathic age as they did in the cognitive era? What if *empathy really does matter* for the economy of the future?

We left the Agricultural Revolution in the dust. The Industrial Revolution is in our rear-view mirror. We're closing the book on the Knowledge Revolution. As we move through this latest Technological Revolution, a new asset class is emerging: empathy. As the new asset class, empathy has the potential to topple our fundamental ideas about assets and classes. Empathy will be the asset class to end all asset classes. According to Rifkin, "Empathy is a communion of kindred spirits, and it's elicited in a temporal and spatial zone that transcends distinctions based on social status."[69]

CHAPTER 7

The Economic Endgame:
Empathy, Innovation,
and the Bottom Line

Innovation has been the lifeblood of our economy, and human progress overall, since before we dragged our knuckles out of the caves. We like to claim it as a modern phenomenon, but it's as old as cooking with fire, rolling a wheel, and fashioning an arrowhead. Today's tools are different, but the idea is the same. The Hamilton Project puts it this way:

> *Innovation is the process of discovering new ideas and realizing those ideas at large scale, changing the ways we live and work. Innovation has transformed the American economy through the development of automobiles and highways, airplanes, telecommunications, and the Internet, all of which have made it progressively easier for businesses to market their products globally and connect their best workers to one another. Innovations like these drive economic growth by helping businesses produce more with less—progress that is measured as rising productivity. As businesses and workers become more productive, the prices of goods and services fall and workers' wages rise, improving our standard of living.*[70]

BARRIERS TO INNOVATION

As we saw earlier, innovation, measured by total factor productivity, is growing at a snail's pace. And real innovation? Innovation with soul appears to be eluding us almost completely these days.

There are many possible explanations for our inability to innovate. Economic experts are all over it. Here is just a sample of where we typically lay blame for lack of innovation:

- A regulatory environment that creates barriers to innovation

- A decrease in investment in research and development by the federal government

- Too few students pursuing advanced degrees in fields critical to innovation, such as STEM

- Innovative effort going to fixing our past mistakes, such as cleaning up the environment

All of the above are hotly debated and probably will be for a long time, but there is one thing that has received lots of attention and general consensus: As a society, we have become more scared, less brave. We are more risk averse. Everyone wants to help you with that, once and for all. Consultants. Authors. Innovators. Disruptors! Even Disney movies are telling us how to be brave. We've been here before.

Despite the fact that we have more physical capital and cognitive resources than ever before, we're more fearful than ever. What gives? Why didn't we believe Stuart Smalley the first time he modeled for us on *Saturday Night Live*: "I'm good enough, smart enough…and doggone it, people like me!"?

Maybe it is time to reframe the issue. Because we know that more stuff and brainpower hasn't gotten us there, maybe innovation is not a regulatory or educational issue after all. Maybe it is an emotional issue that requires that we put a premium on a new asset class—the asset class of empathy. And maybe that's the deficit we should spend more time analyzing and fixing. Let's give it a try.

PUTTING THE "SOUL" IN INNOVATION

Can you imagine how empathy affects what flows through an organization and supports innovation? Innovation requires change, which is hard for people even when it's good. Change brings fear, loss, frustration, and even rewiring of our brains. Empathy gives us the courage to move through all that together.

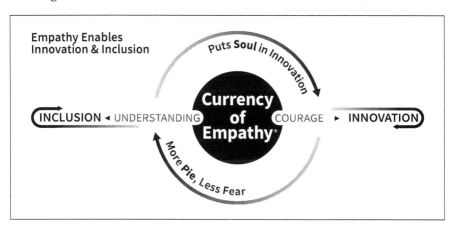

And maybe empathy solves another problem. Even though we are producing more, this newfound abundance is not distributed equally.[71] Inequality is at an all-time high, and if it doesn't affect you now, it will. People have noted that inequality is the beginning of how nations fail.[72] Many people do not consider inequality a problem of innovation. Rather, they say, innovation is in the business of making more of something. Distribution is the government's problem.

But here's a radical thought. What if empathy didn't just give us more, but solved that age-old quandary between growth and distribution? What if empathy didn't give us just innovation, but innovation *with soul*?

The best kind of innovation is done with soul. This is not inconsistent with making money, but it serves a higher purpose than quick profits for a select few—it leads to a *more abundant world for everyone*. Innovation with soul is inclusive in its process. It creates "with" rather than "for." Innovation with soul creates products that put the power of health in consumers' hands rather than profiting from our diseases. Innovation with soul designs new ways to increase access to vital things like education, rather than trying to justify, one more time with feeling, the return on the current average cost of ~$140K for a private college education in the US (not including room and board).

How about education for free? That's right, for free. It's already happening. The biggest information product in the world—Wikipedia—is made by volunteers for free, abolishing the encyclopedia business and depriving the advertising industry of an estimated $3 billion a year in revenue. Massive open online courses, or MOOCs, take off where Wikipedia ends. What does it cost to take a MOOC? Nothing. Who can do it? Anyone with access to the Internet, all over the world. How will all of this upend the traditional model of the university? We've only just begun to imagine. How will these new models contribute to an abundant world for everyone? It's not completely clear, but it feels like the right direction.

Innovation with soul is good for everyone and forever (or at least as far out as we can imagine). And empathy is how you get it. Empathy is what helps us include as many people as possible in these decisions. *Real* inclusion. Not just lip service to women and minorities, with an eye toward "marketing" to children. Real inclusion means valuing the ideas and needs of all workers, unlike today's productivity quotas that leave people resentful, exploited, or just hopeless because they never truly have a place at the table.

EMPATHY'S ROLE IN INCLUSION

How can empathy support real inclusion? Let's frame this emotionally again. Including other people can be scary. It can threaten our identity, our sense of who we are, and our place in the world. It's not our fault; it's our evolutionary habit from competing for resources in a world of scarcity.

Moving from habitual fear to including people who are different from us starts with acknowledging the possibility of abundance and seeing each other more clearly; it starts with empathy. It requires that we find sameness between us to navigate our perceived differences. Without feeling understood and valued, people will opt out emotionally, if not physically, which is exactly what's happening today in most organizations.

It helps that innovation supports inclusion by growing the pie. The bigger the pie, the more abundance, the less scarcity and fear, and the easier it is to include others. Inclusion brings diverse views, creativity, and everyone all in…in short, inclusion brings *real soul* to innovation. It's a virtuous cycle, with empathy as the intermediary—the currency. Empathy. Is. The. Missing. Link. No amount of leaning into the current systems is going to solve our problems of inclusion and innovation. Not for women. And not for men.

What happens when we leave empathy out? You may get innovation, but it probably won't be innovation with soul. Not all innovation is good. This we know. The latest snack chip may be considered innovative, despite the fact that it makes us sick and addicted. But what happens is we (or even more, our children and grandchildren) are left to foot the bill for rising rates of obesity. What good was that innovation and that company's profit in the first place? And how might things have been different had a hands-on parent been included in this decision affecting future generations? Would he or she have felt okay signing off on Jacked Doritos or promoting research "proving" Coke isn't bad for our kids, without pangs of conscience?

Instead of stewarding empathy, the current system stewards the opposite. It is a vicious cycle we've created by putting money and stuff and the disorder it all throws off (entropy) at the center of how we allocate our time.

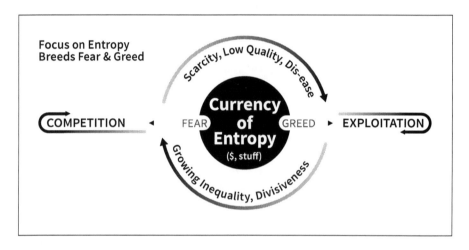

Rather than innovation, our work throws off exploitation (e.g., of overworked, undervalued employees; of unsuspecting customers; of suppliers under the thumb of behemoth companies; of taxpayers left to foot the bill for banks that are too big to fail). Forget about inclusion. It's every man for himself in this competitive environment. It breeds scarcity, low quality, disease, growing inequality, and divisiveness. The overwhelming atmosphere is of fear and distrust. It doesn't feel good. Maybe this sounds like where you work...

So what? They call it work because they pay you. So what if work doesn't feel good and takes up most of our waking hours? Shouldn't we just suck it up? Isn't it working for the economy? If we lift our heads up from work for a moment, then we see...not so much. We remember the lack of innovation no one seems to be able to solve. Slowing growth and profitability. Lack of employee engagement. We see that something is amiss in the economy. It has been for a while. And we're not going to solve it by doing the same things we've done before.

So, what if we tried something different, like focusing on empathy? Would the results be different? What would happen? We have some clues.

EMPATHY IMPROVES THE BOTTOM LINE

Empathy is hitting the bottom line in ways people have only just begun to try to measure. According to the Global Empathy Index recently developed by The Empathy Business, the top 10 businesses among 160 generated 50% more net income per employee than the bottom 10. The index analyzed factors such as CEO approval ratings, diversity, how well companies treat workers, and effectiveness of communication with customers.[73]

In our own research using the Currency of Empathy® diagnostic with clients, we see similar results. High scores in areas that support rather than thwart empathic development (e.g., meaningful work, growth-oriented professional development, work-life balance) are correlated with innovation statistics (e.g., revenue growth and percentage of new products and services).[74]

It's all very new. So new that there aren't yet reams of data specifically connecting empathy, innovation, inclusion, and the bottom line for organizations. Data can be so encouraging. We wish there were more already. What we have ad nauseam are data proving the old way doesn't work. That's the thing about data. Data are historical. Data tell a story about what happened in the past. Data tell us who we used to be. Or who we have become over time, until now.

Imagining who we could become in the future is more of an art, requiring a combination of creativity, common sense, news ways of looking at old data, and new ways to collect new data…from everyone. Including you

But all in all, we are encouraged. Because the leaders of the future can be different from the leaders of the past. Not just on the surface. But from the inside out and upside down.

CHAPTER 8

Upending the
Leadership Pyramid

To review: Leadership as usual gives lip service to empathy, but doesn't embody it. Yet empathy is required to move forward in the new economy. So, what does the New Leader look like? Is it *you*? Let's see.

If we revisit what leadership really is and keep empathy in mind, we get a vastly different picture. The evolution of an interconnected, inclusive, co-creative network is starting to make the old style of leadership obscene. It's turning the pointy pyramid upside down, and emerging leaders find it a relief not be so alone anymore.

Leadership Is NOT	Leadership Is
Lonely at the Top	Dialogue
A Monologue	Inclusive
An Individual Sport	For Wise, Whole People
For Workaholics	Co-Creative
Competitive	Valuable
Compensated	Jazz

LEADERSHIP IS A TWO-WAY CONVERSATION

Leadership can only take place when two or more people are gathered and engaged in **dialogue.** It's a two-way conversation in which everyone is included. It's not a boss giving everyone else a heads-up. It's not us pretending to pay attention, while fiddling with our phones. It's a boss genuinely open to including other points of view or, better yet, a partnership in which everyone's view contributes to an answer better than any one person could design. It is through this dialogue that leadership can truly be inclusive.

LEADERSHIP IS INCLUSIVE

Leadership must be **inclusive,** not because that's the nice way, but because otherwise, we'll have all the wrong answers. Your customers are more diverse than ever; having a boardroom that represents those different points of view will help you know their needs, imagine their hopes, and hit their bull's-eye. The days of *Father Knows Best* are over. We've been there and done that already, haven't we?

Even the smartest room full of white men cannot understand what it is to be Black or a woman in this country, yet they invent for us, make decisions for us, and even tell us what to think. Empathy is not presuming what other people feel and need in their absence and projecting emotions and solutions onto them. So lack of women and Blacks in leadership means that roughly 65% of the puzzle is missing—just *missing*—from the boardroom before we even consider socioeconomics. Collectively, that's pretty stupid.

And money makes the picture even more myopic. Who benefits from new technologies these days, anyway? Not everyone. Egg freezing? Cryogenics? Commuter spaceships? Step right up, 1%. You have a FastPass+.[75]

LEADERSHIP IS NOT ABOUT PROFIT

Leadership is not about utilizing people and manipulating systems to make money. The raison d'etre is not profit. Real leaders don't need to be egregiously compensated, because the privilege of being a leader is inherently **valuable.** Real leadership is about making your world a better place, inside the office and out. It's about knowing that someone will be better off because of the work you did today. It's about doing something meaningful for your fellow humans, while engaging empathically with your team. This is the compensation that matters. That's a good day's work, and we know it. Profits are simply how we FUND that work. Nothing more. Nothing less.

IT'S ABOUT WISDOM

Leadership benefits from the **wisdom that comes from living a whole life.** Real leaders lean into home and encourage their team to do the same. Because they understand the value that human authenticity brings. Burned-out executives in corner offices haven't even had time to take care of themselves much less anyone else, so how could they possibly help us grow? What have they learned other than how to climb the ladder in record time? Whom have they loved? What have they risked and lost? If it's no one and nothing, how can they possibly relate to us vulnerable human beings?

LEADERSHIP IS CO-CREATIVE

Leadership is not competitive but **co-creative.** It's not about fighting over a shrinking prize, but imagining new ones, with enough for everyone. This is the win-win that Rifkin was talking about. It's admitting that no one of us has all of the answers, but together we do. It's admitting that you can't do anything really important alone. It's being humble and vulnerable enough to listen as much as or more than you talk. It's not being so married to your ideas. It's putting an inspiration out there, letting someone else play with it, build on it, and change it. Then, being able to incorporate that new idea back into your life, rather than rejecting it like a transplanted foreign tissue.

Co-creation is making something better than you could have ever done alone. There is some mystery to it. It's an adventure. It's art, which author Madeleine L'Engle has said is "channeling cosmos into the chaos."[76] And we still have plenty of chaos to resolve. So, true leaders work together and make the world a better place from wherever they sit.

LEADERS ARE NOT LONERS

Finally, a lonely leader is an oxymoron. Is no one willing to keep you company when the paycheck doesn't depend on it? That's not leadership, at the top or anywhere.

Have you ever had the pleasure to watch a long-standing **jazz** band? That's a type of co-creative art we get to witness in real time. So much preparation goes into what they do, but leading a jazz band doesn't look like work. It looks like fun. Activist and actor Wendell Pierce has said jazz allows people to be an "individual within form"[77]—that form providing a greater common purpose. That's what real leadership feels like, too.

Doesn't this sound like some of the best leaders you've ever known? If you're lucky enough to have known some, that is. Leaders with empathy are leaders we follow. We don't check out in the presence of those leaders. Instead, we bring our all to our work. Full employee engagement would be a great start toward improving the bottom line, not to mention improving innovation. Can you see it? Can you see how leaders with empathy encourage us to be brave enough to move through the change that innovation requires?

LEADERSHIP IS BECOMING EMOTIONAL

Don't get distracted by positional authority, which too often has little to do with leadership. There are unpaid bloggers or church deacons who are more like these New Leaders than are many CEOs. But we're getting ahead of ourselves. Let's check in with the leadership experts.

First, Daniel Goleman. Although Peter Salovey and John Mayer were the first to coin the term "emotional intelligence" (EI), Goleman made it popular in his 1995 book of the same name.[78] That's when this *radical* idea that emotional skills are as important as IQ became more mainstream. Though the details of EI are still emerging, the overall concept makes a lot of sense. Our emotional lives matter. Our feelings matter. They matter to our personal lives and our professional success. This is the stuff of life.

Emotional intelligence researchers like Goleman remind us that leadership relies on mobilizing human skills like empathy—now more than ever. He says, "The most effective leaders, we've long known, have more competence in emotional intelligence. It's not your college degrees or IQ that make you an outstanding leader, but emotional intelligence abilities."[79]

Leaders who get the best results tend to show more strength in the key competencies of emotional intelligence, in particular: self-awareness, self-management, empathy, and social effectiveness.

Successful leaders in the future will look and feel very different. This new way of leadership will affect all of us, sooner or later.

It's just a matter of time.

✳

Clearing Up Our Mix-Ups about Home, Especially Quality Time

CHAPTER 9

Mix-Up No. 2
We Need Quantity Time at Work but Quality Time at Home

"Historical fact: people stopped being human in 1913. That was the year Henry Ford put his cars on rollers and made his workers adopt the speed of the assembly line. At first, workers rebelled. They quit in droves, unable to accustom their bodies to the new pace of the age. Since then, however, the adaptation has been passed down; we've all inherited it to some degree, so that we plug right into joysticks and remotes, to repetitive motions of a hundred kinds."
—Jeffrey Eugenides, Middlesex

There is still another mix-up to address. We've discussed how work isn't working. But these days, neither is home. Because we have a mix-up about time. We still believe that we need "quantity time" at work but only "quality time" at home. This is *Mix-Up No. 2*.

To review: The world is changing and empathy seems suddenly important. We need empathy to survive in this new economy. How do we get empathy? We develop affective empathy in relationships. The more significant the relationship, the greater the potential for growth. Children rely on their parents to grow their affective empathy. For parents, there is no greater chance to continue their empathic development than through relationships with their children. Which starts at home.

Yes, at home. *Home* is where babies nap and eat and play and even cry. Then they grow into toddlers who need to taste, pull up to stand, and fall down. Then they are preschoolers whose job it is to learn how to be okay on their own, without mom and dad, so they can relate to other people and the world. It's exhausting work, and they really love a hug when they get home. Then they are schoolkids who want to show you their umpteenth painting, celebrate their spelling test, or just cry with someone who loves them because their best friend broke their heart today. The children are at home, but *our work is "outside the home."*

Affective empathy is also cultivated with our spouses, partners, lovers, parents, grandparents, best friends, and other close relationships. These relationships are also found in the home or in that sphere of life considered personal. There isn't enough time for hands-on caring when we work. There isn't enough time for work if our hands/heads/hearts are busy parenting or attending to our loved ones. So what do we do? What do we do to reduce this dilemma? We tell ourselves stories. Like this one. *We need quality time at home and quantity time at work.*

The hard-earned prize of the feminist revolution was the opportunity to work "outside the home." Today, women work and raise families in droves, bearing down at the intersection of *existing paradigms of work* and *traditional notions of family.* Work is where economic activity with financial benefit occurs. Home is a separate physical sphere where our personal life dwells. We cannot be in both places at once. Today, most parents spend the majority of their waking hours at work. Early mornings, evenings, nights, and weekends are usually spent at home.

Unfortunately, we are living in a society that makes it difficult to work outside the home while cultivating affective empathy *in* the home.

We are stuck in an untenable position, and it is costing us. Home hurts. Work hurts. The world hurts. Everyone is losing.

How did we get here?

THE FACTORY-PRODUCTION MODEL

To understand our modern work-home paradigm, let's hit some highlights from just the last ~100 years:

- **Back on the farm,** work and family were intertwined. Women worked in the home and men in the fields. Extended family was there, to tend to and to be cared for. Work and family were integrated. Balance depended on how quickly babies could grow and help. There wasn't as much time or space for babies to develop "separation anxiety," a term coined in the ~1920s.

- **The industrial revolution** brought a lot of change and some progress to everything from manufacturing to education. Efficiency was key, and people were brought together in factories, towns, and schools to produce more: better, faster, cheaper products for mass use. There is no doubt it raised the average standard of living. It also separated work and family. Given the need for brawn at work as well as the biological reality that only women could give birth and nurse, men went to work and women mostly stayed home. Extended families were also separated as people transferred to the cities for work. Things moved quickly. Henry Ford introduced the Model T on October 2, 1908. In 1940, the 40-hour workweek went into effect as mandated by the Fair Labor Standards Act.

- **The knowledge economy** ushered in opportunities that were more intellectual than physical, so it made sense that educated women had lots to contribute by the time the feminists of the 1960s and '70s set the table for them. So work "outside of the home" became commonplace for women, but also ignited "Mommy Wars." Still, many mommies went to work, leaving a void at home that was filled by the outsourcing of childcare.

• **The most recent technology and communication revolution,** in which the iPhone and social media increasingly linked us 24/7 to this networked economy across time and space, brought enormous potential for work flexibility—but also no rest for the weary. We are on, all the time. Some of it is driven by work cultures, some by addiction. The result is the same. Even when we are with our loved ones, we or they are staring at screens.

• **Last but not least, we are what we count.** Currency matters, and our way of counting what's valuable has become increasingly disconnected from what's naturally inside of us or even beneath our feet. The emergence of currency as a way of exchanging work other than barter was a huge shift in how we humans could spend our time and even view the future. It liberated us to specialize and progress. It offered some hope for the future. Suddenly, value could be securely stored and fairly shared over time and across physical circumstances. Fair currency bound us to each other in faith that we could share talents and be better together.

Since 1971 the value of our currency is no longer bound to the physical world (e.g., tied to gold), but rather is determined by fiat—manipulated, compounded, and hoarded. We make money with money. Some people think that's a bad habit. We can see why. These manipulations can be powerful tools used by a few to affect the many. And the global fluctuations in currency values do affect us, a lot. They affect our emotional stability, identity, sense of self-worth, values, how we show up at work and at home, and how we vote. They reach right into our inner world…our conscience and our hope and faith in the future. When the stock market goes up, we feel good. When it goes down, we worry. What we count matters. It's one of main ways we keep score, and no one wants to be a loser.

So, the currency yoke and factory production work model persist, despite technology that makes working across time and space more possible than ever. Most of us must still abide by the 40-hour workweek (at least) and time clocks, and second jobs, and bosses who judge us by time spent at the office.

In the US especially, there simply isn't time to care for kids, aging parents, or even ourselves. The US ranks near the bottom of work-family balance across the globe.

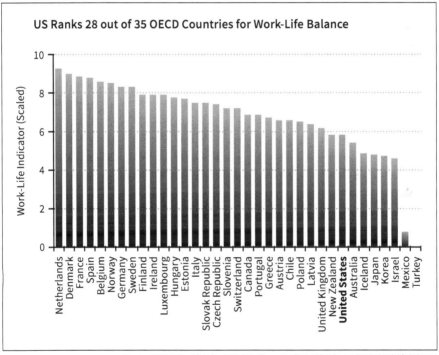

Source: OECD Better Life Index, 2017, http://www.oecdbetterlifeindex.org/topics/work-life-balance/

The mix-up starts early. The US ranks last in the developed world for paid parental leave. *Last.*

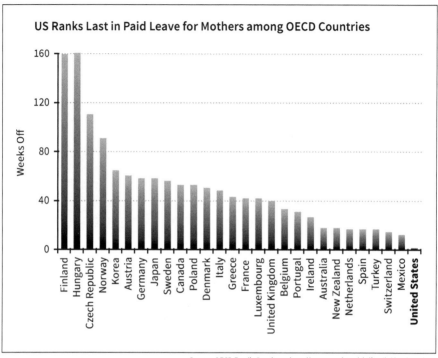

Source: OECD Family Database, http://www.oecd.org/els/family/database.htm

As of the writing of this book, we are one of only three countries left in the world that do not guarantee paid maternity leave. The others are Papua New Guinea and Oman. The closest thing we have is the Family and Medical Leave Act (FMLA), which became law in 1993 and allows qualified employees to take 12 weeks of *unpaid,* job-protected leave for specific family and medical reasons. Unpaid, which not many people can afford.

Sadly, if we want to keep our jobs, there is often little choice but to step *out* of our homes just as we should be gearing up for the work of affective empathy. Instead of being physically present with our children during this critical juncture, we are forced to significantly outsource the caring of our children at a very young age.

SANDBERG WAS RIGHT ABOUT TIME

By suggesting women could achieve more if they were more willing to "lean in" to the male-dominated work spaces, Sheryl Sandberg may have rubbed many the wrong way. But she did get one thing right. If you want to *lead* in today's world, you do need to lean in—with all your might. The more time you spend at the office, the more likely you are to succeed. Workaholism is your secret weapon.

Harvard economist Claudia Goldin has studied the pay gap between men and women extensively.[80] Her research shows a positive correlation between time at work and salary. The more time people give to work according to a fixed schedule and the more continuous that time is, the more people get paid. Conversely, people who work fewer and more flexible hours end up making significantly less money than their counterparts. This is especially true in those institutions that wield the most power and money—the corporate, financial, and legal worlds. While explicit gender bias and differences in working style are often cited as the reasons for the pay disparities women face, Goldin illustrates that "on call" schedules, "face time," client demands, and group meetings are the factors that disadvantage workers most.

What does this mean for leadership? Assuming that pay is associated with level of responsibility, we can conclude that leadership is most accessible to those who have the most time to give to work. Leadership is most accessible to those who do not periodically step out of the workforce, decrease their work hours, or work flexibly. So, it makes sense that parents who are involved in the hands-on caring of children are, more often than not, the ones left behind. Parents, usually women, who remain connected to home by guilt and love and need, parents who don't have the stomach to completely walk away, parents who are doing the hard work of affective empathy development, are typically not the ones groomed and chosen for leadership positions.

CHILD DEVELOPMENT IS ALSO RIGHT ABOUT TIME

Jean Piaget, the famous Swiss psychologist, studied the role of object permanence in child development. Object permanence is the understanding that objects continue to exist even if they can't be seen. It is a significant milestone in the cognitive development of children that occurs between 9 and 18 months of age. Prior to this time, babies are unable to even think about things they cannot see. To the infant, that which he cannot see does not even exist. The most significant "object" for a baby is, of course, the parent. But without this early ability to keep the parent in mind while the parent is not present, long absences can have a significant impact on a child's future ability to keep the other in mind. This ability to keep others in mind is foundational to empathy. Quantity of time is exactly what infants need to develop healthy empathy.

AFTER INFANCY

Family leave is only a partial solution—because infancy is only the beginning. What happens after the first year when our babies start to look less helpless? They toddle, from home base out into the world and back again. It's like tag, and parents are the safety zone. Then they are preschoolers who learn how to exist in the world as separate human beings. Teachers become a new safety zone, but this emotional work is exhausting. It's not at all easy for young children to do much less for the 40-hour workweek we often impose on them. It's exhausting work, and they really love a hug when they get home. Then they are schoolkids, and just when we think they don't need us, they do. Their need shows up when you least expect it—after a devastating fight with a friend, a health issue, or a teacher who is so unfair. It's hard to know exactly when these needs will arise, so we have to be at the ready somehow. Fortunately or unfortunately, metabolizing these experiences in a generative way is not trivial emotional or cognitive work. It's work that requires deep relationships, and yes, empathy.

By some accounts, teenagers need us even more than our nine-year-old does. The healthy teenager is working hard to separate and individuate on her path to becoming an adult. It's a critical time, as we may recall from our own teenage years, and being available goes a long way.

NEUROSCIENTISTS ARE RIGHT ABOUT TIME

Evolutionary biologists agree that the seeds of empathy were planted with the beginning of maternal care in mammals millions of years ago. Maternal care has been a hallmark of Homo sapiens for 200,000 years, which is a *long time* to work on our DNA.[81] In order for her baby to survive, mom needed a way to read and respond to her infant's cues. She also needed support from others, so she worked hard to build social networks.[82] Empathy became her tool. It also became a selective advantage. Though studies examining empathy in infants provide mixed results, it is not beyond the realm of possibility that female Homo sapiens are born more empathic than male Homo sapiens.

But is this the whole story? If caretaking historically led to the natural selection of empathy, what can we say about the impact of parenting within a given lifetime? A lot, actually.

Neuroscientists are now finding that hands-on parenting increases empathy in the brain.[83]

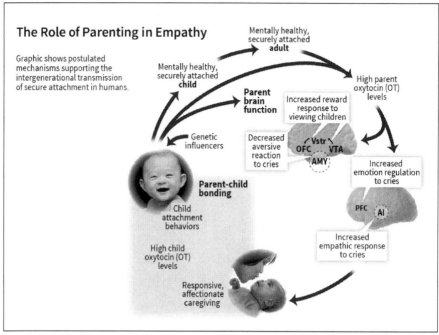

The Role of Parenting in Empathy

Graphic shows postulated mechanisms supporting the intergenerational transmission of secure attachment in humans.

Mentally healthy, securely attached **adult**

Mentally healthy, securely attached **child**

Parent brain function

High parent oxytocin (OT) levels

Increased reward response to viewing children

Genetic influencers

Decreased aversive reaction to cries

Vstr
OFC · VTA
AMY

Increased emotion regulation to cries

Parent-child bonding

Child attachment behaviors

PFC AI

Increased empathic response to cries

High child oxytocin (OT) levels

Responsive, affectionate caregiving

Source: James K. Rilling and Larry Young, "The biology of mammalian parenting and its effect on offspring social development." *Science* 345, no. 6198 (2014): 771-776. Copyright © 2014 by the American Association for the Advancement of Science. Reprinted with permission.

Through hormones, infant cues, and time invested in caretaking, parenting reconfigures our neural networks. In fact, the postpartum period may represent the period of greatest plasticity for the adult human brain. Our grandmothers didn't need *research* to *prove* that caring for kids grows our hearts, but now we do.

Luckily, scientists found new mothers willing to lie down in fMRI machines and reflect on their infants so they could witness empathy in action. While we wonder how these moms got themselves to the lab when we can barely brush our teeth, we're grateful for their service. The resulting fMRI images show activity (blood flow) in the areas of the brain associated with empathy.[84]

By testing their blood and saliva (thanks again, moms), they could also see an elevation of the hormones regulating empathic responses (e.g., prolactin, oxytocin) in pregnancy, during nursing, and with skin-to-skin contact with their babies. These studies showed that the more hands-on, interactive behavior that parents engaged in, the higher their oxytocin levels. The studies also found correlations not just with the type of behaviors parents engaged in but also in the amount of time parents spent with their children. Empathy takes time. *Empathy is a contact sport.* The more time, the more contact, the more empathy.

We appreciate scientific inquiry and the hard work that goes into these studies. But if that's not your thing, try this: If you're a parent, think about when you first held your baby. Think about a warm hug from your mom when you were a kid. There you go. You got it. Quantity time with our children gives us a second chance at remembering empathy. From a biological perspective, there is no substitute for this time.

Just a quick note: If an increase in testosterone is what you are looking for, time at work is one way to get it. A new compelling study showed that when women playacted exercising power over another, testosterone hormone levels rose.[85] While the impact of higher testosterone on women caring for children is not clear, studies suggest that higher testosterone levels in men are associated with lower sensitivity to infant cues.[86]

Family leave, flexible work schedules, job sharing, and other attempts at giving people better work-life balance are only so helpful. While these solutions make sense in theory, they don't address the deeper structural issues keeping work and home separate. How can we spend time at home when our success at work depends on time?

And who wants to be home anyway, when there are no lights in the village? It can be so very lonely.

*

CHAPTER 10

Bad Dreams at Home— No Lights in the Village

The landscape of home has changed significantly, especially over the last 50 years or so. What did home used to look like? Pregnancy and nursing ensured mom always had a starring role. Dad played best supporting actor, which meant many things, including hunting, going to war, going to meetings… but, until recently, not much hands-on parenting. Home was a matriarchy. Women ruled. Outside the home was patriarchy. Men ruled.

But in this matriarchy where women ruled, at least women ruled together. There was company. There was a village. There had to be because raising kids is difficult, complex work. Evolutionary biologists suggest that this need for a village created another bump up in women's empathic tendencies. To gather a village, women had to know how to organize and bring people together. It was an essential, established practice that ensured the continuation of the human race.

And then came the suburbs of the 1950s.

Though our ancestors knew that raising kids alone was impossible, by mid-century, the village model was beginning to disappear. We moved away from our extended families, dads went to work outside the neighborhood, but at least moms had each other…and their martinis. Isolation in the suburbs separated people from their neighbors, and the evolving land-scape of industry meant more geographical dissolution of the extended family. Betty Friedan documented this sense of growing anomie faced by the American housewife in *The Feminine Mystique*. A review of this feminist classic reveals that it was less a message of "we want to get out into the world," and more "get me out of this hellhole, ASAP." That's right. The village devolved into the suburban lead-parent model, where one person was left alone in the room with the job of ushering helpless, dependent life into the world. It was too much to bear and women started fleeing in droves.

Can you blame them? For the stay-at-home parent entrusted with nothing less than a vulnerable human life, this lack of partnership with another invested person—*someone with skin in the game*—is nothing less than cruel. It makes it difficult to access the empathy in the room, resulting in fusion and resentment. Rather than empathy between parents, there grows anger and disconnect. Alone in a bubble with a needy baby, toddler, or child, and with little time for self-care, the lead parent becomes depleted of empathy for self. Studies show that postpartum depres-sion rates plummet for women when a supportive partner is available. We wonder if it wasn't a coincidence that women ran away to the office just as the isolation of suburban living was moving firmly into place. And today, when neighborhoods are virtual ghost towns during the day, how can we blame anyone for choosing work over home?

And that's exactly what many women are doing. In her sociological study of work and home, Arlie Hochschild offered further support for this theory in her book *Time Bind*. She found that when given the opportunity to work flexibly, women preferred time at the office to time at home. Work was perceived as a place of belonging, while home was perceived as a place of demands.[87] Home is repelling parents as much as work is demanding their time. As a result, the birthplace of affective empathy is at risk. And so are our well-being, health, and sanity. Because our guilt is eating us alive.

GUILT

Before our children have words, our empathic communication is body to body. It is based on touch, sound, smell, taste, and gaze. We experience our infant's emotions and reflect them back nonverbally. This nonverbal and largely unconscious dance of affective empathy sets the foundation for attachment—their attachment to us and our attachment to them. Yes, it's a two-way street. As neuroscientists can attest, when we attach to our kids, our empathy is humming along. But without adequate parental leave, we are all too often forced to interrupt this dance. Then what happens?

Unless you are a psychopath, the guilt sets in. And it's usually hell. "It feels like you are cutting off your arm," is how one mother we know put it when she had to leave her newborn to go back to work. Understandably, we cannot survive in this position for long. When we can no longer bear the pain, something must be done. If it's feasible, some parents (usually moms) ramp down at work or even quit. Interestingly, after decades of decline, stay-at-home motherhood is now on the rise.[88]

But what if we can't afford to quit because we are a single parent trying to climb out of poverty? What if we don't want to quit because we love our work and it feels like oxygen? Or what if we didn't go through 12 years of neurosurgery training to drop out now? What if we are slated to become the next CEO of a major technology company, the first woman ever? What happens then?

One thing we often do is take down guilt itself. We criticize people for making us feel guilty. We recently witnessed this on International Women's

Day during a speech by a CEO giving women advice on how to become a leader. She told a story about a three-week business trip she had to take when her daughter was seven months old. She lamented that people made her feel guilty about leaving her daughter and urged the audience, "Don't let them make you feel guilty." She couldn't get the words out, though. She started coughing and had to take a break for water. Perhaps guilt remains for her. No matter how we try to think our way out of it, the uncomfortable feeling remains. While people can shame us all they want, no one can make us feel guilty; we do that all on our own.

Has guilt always been bad or has it just gotten a bad rap lately? Generations of grandmothers can't be wrong. Guilt can be useful. Shame, not so much. They are different. Shame is socially constructed and imposed from the outside in—a power play that keeps others in line because of the threat of humiliation or worse, separation from society. We're social animals, built to live relationally, so shame is a big deal. Shame is a powerful tool. It has been wielded throughout the ages for less-than-noble purposes, such as retaining power. One long-standing, widespread example is shame used in patriarchal cultures to keep women in the home and out of power. We also use shame when we scold men to stop those unconscious biases. And we use shame against people's racist language. Shame is a sharp tool to that end. But generally, it is not effective.

Guilt, on the other hand, comes from the inside out. The guilt we feel has honest origins. It is a signal from our unconscious—our bodies, actually—when something isn't working for us. It is to our unconscious what physical pain is to our body. Its tracks are laid early, during the affective dance between parent and baby. It can be painful if not untenable, especially if we can't do anything to resolve the guilt-inducing conflict (e.g., when we can't be home because we need to spend long hours away just to put food on the table). But guilt can be a good sign. It means that our affective empathy is intact. It is also the reason that ignoring our guilt never really works, no matter how inconvenient it is.

THE STORIES WE TELL OURSELVES

Society has convenient narratives to salve our conscience and relieve us from guilt. These stories become the coping mechanisms we use to try to resolve, numb, or ignore the pain of the disconnect between our thoughts and our behaviors. Cognitive scientists call the resulting strain we feel "cognitive dissonance." Wikipedia describes cognitive dissonance this way: "The psychological tension that occurs when one holds mutually exclusive beliefs or attitudes and that often motivates people to modify their thoughts or behaviors in order to reduce the tension."[89]

The biggest story we tell ourselves is this: It's okay if we spend quantity time at work, as long as we spend quality time at home. Instead of giving parents—both mother and father—adequate maternity and paternity leave so that they can be with their children unencumbered during these crucial formative months, we normalize the outsourcing of care. We applaud calls for cheaper daycare, rather than question the implicit message we are sending: It's okay if we spend a large quantity of time at work, if the limited time we have at home is *quality*.

The Myth That Quality Trumps Quantity

How do we know this is a myth?

A cursory review of the fundamental tenets of child development clarifies the amount of time children need from their parents for healthy emotional development. The more the better, especially early on. Part of this need is explained by the fact that a child's sense of time is different from how adults view time. In early childhood, children cannot distinguish between mommy or daddy leaving for two hours and mommy or daddy leaving forever. We know this from the elevated cortisol levels of children separated early from their parents. Baron-Cohen sums it up by saying that time with our children early on gives them an "internal pot of gold" of healthy empathy. [90]

Recent neuroscientific studies measuring the impact of parenting on parental empathy mirror the impact on children. What kind of parenting actually increases empathy in the parent? Turns out, it is the same kind of parenting that children require for their own empathy development. These studies show a positive correlation between time spent in contact with the baby and an increase in parental empathy, confirming that children need our time—in quantity, not just quality.

But if we do a gut check, we don't need these studies. Our guilt tells us the truth—the guilt we are forced to swallow when we walk away from our kids before they and we are ready. Here are some ways society tries to help us deal with our cognitive dissonance vis-à-vis children:

> **Explicit:** "XYZ is the best daycare."
> **Implicit:** "My child is being taken care of so I don't need to worry. I can go to work." We know that this is a common mix-up. While 88% of parents are convinced their daycare is very good to excellent, those who study child development rate the vast majority of daycares as fair. [91]

> **Explicit:** "My kid isn't in daycare. My kid is at school."
> **Implicit:** "School is providing my child with education, which is more important than what I can provide. So it's okay if I go to work." The problem is that the learning that kids need to be doing at this age is not cognitive (e.g., ABCs, 123s, colors), it's affective (i.e., I feel safe and warm and loved).

Explicit: "Daycare is the right decision because I want my kid to grow up independent. I want my child to grow up being comfortable with all sorts of people."
Implicit: "Daycare is better for my child than I am. So it's okay if he is there without me." The problem is that studies show that attachment to a primary caretaker is what will give a child the ability to become resilient in different kinds of situations. Too many caretakers too early on makes children dependent, not independent.

Explicit: "Leaving your baby will feel like cutting off your arm. Just move through it, and it will get better."
Implicit: "If I don't think about it, eventually the pain will go away. Work will once again become manageable." For many parents, it doesn't actually get better. Most parents just become more numb.

Explicit: "This daycare is fantastic because it gives children 'motherly love.'" Or "The nanny loves the kids like another grandma."
Implicit: "The daycare/nanny is a better mother than I am. So it's okay if they are with her." Grandma would beg to differ. The kids know the difference, too, even in the best cases. Children want their parents. Maybe there is no such thing as "pay to love."[92]

These are just some examples. But collectively, they come under the umbrella of a big, modern mix-up: the idea that it's okay if we spend *quantity* time at work as long as we spend *quality* time at home. Child-development findings—better yet, a conversation with your grandma—would reveal these claims to be illogical at best and absurd at worst.

But guilt is a powerful thing. And it can cause us to accept fake news rather than feel guilty.

Yet the Myth Continues

So powerful is this need to resolve our untenable position that many industries work diligently to support this myth. One group with which many are familiar is the teacher/doctor/big pharma/researcher industrial complex. This complex promotes psychotropic medications for our children to settle them quickly, when what many really need is an academic setting that is more developmentally appropriate, or simply more attention at home.

And then there is the academic/journalist industrial complex. This group is known for publishing and reporting studies supporting the quality/quantity mix-up, regardless of the rigor with which the studies were conducted. In March of 2015, one such study, which concluded that time spent doing hands-on parenting had little impact on child outcomes, was widely reported by major outlets such as the *Washington Post*, the *Guardian* and NBC News. The study was pulled only after Justin Wolfers of the *New York Times* decided to take a closer look, determining that poor data made the study's conclusion essentially a nonfinding.

In a follow-up, David Leonhardt shed some light on what we had just witnessed:

> But the notion that time doesn't matter for parenting makes almost exactly as much sense as the notion that time doesn't matter for, say, journalism. Do you think a reporter who spends an hour on the beat will usually produce as good a story as someone who spends 10? And we shouldn't let academics off the hook here, either. They have the same ingrained bias as we journalists do.[93]

That's right. The people doing the studies and writing the stories are parents who are also stuck. They need this mix-up as much as the rest of us.

*

CHAPTER 11

Recurring Nightmares at Home

When most of our day is spent at work, we become time poor at home and are forced to take shortcuts. We have learned to parent efficiently. We have also learned to redefine our parenting work to look much more like the work at the office—a place where we are judged on performance. The result? Hyperparenting. You know it. It's all the rage these days. We (over)schedule our kids, check grades online, and do everything else the *Tiger Mother*[94] book tells us to do. What little time we have we use to ensure our kids' competitive edge in the world. There is little chance for happenstance. There is no time to listen. To be quiet. To be. Our empathy is taking another hit.

What happens when we treat our children like projects? We lose sight of who they and we are. We end up overlooking what child development experts tell us about the importance of play in healthy emotional development, and insist our children practice their Suzuki instrument at age four. Our angst about the future professional success of our children keeps us from questioning schools and doctors who prescribe psychotropic medication that our children may not need. We participate in the odd, now socially sanctioned practice of redshirting—flunking our kid to ensure that they are bigger and smarter when it comes to time for college. We force preschools to phase out separation programs, because parents no longer have time for that, even though getting that wrong is correlated with anxiety and depression later in life. We create testing environments at school to match the only world we know—where every day is a test that we cannot afford to fail.

This hurts our kids. But it also hurts us. If we are lucky, our kids will do something to get our attention and alert us to the fact that things are not okay. The remedial action for some people who have never done such a thing before often takes the form of leaning out of work. Anne Marie Slaughter did it when her sons were teenagers, which prompted her to write "Why Women Still Can't Have It All" for the *Atlantic*.[95] She struck a chord. It was the best-selling issue ever, proving that work-life balance and male/female equality debates are far from settled. Eventually though, no matter what, even if our kids are quiet about their pain, we usually get the message—when it's too late. No one on their deathbed has ever said, "I wish I had spent more time at the office."

MARRIAGE/RELATIONSHIPS

The machinations of work and family can be tough on marriage and relationships too. So hard that a lot of people just opt out; fewer than half of the children in the US these days are born to married couples.[96] Endless negotiations about time and money and priorities and whose turn it is to get up this time leave us too tired to—*ehm*—empathize with each other a lot of the time. Millennials have been watching us bungle this, and it doesn't look like much fun. They're taking a pass on marriage at an unprecedented rate.[97]

Here is another place we try to apply work practices, especially when things feel desperately out of balance with partners out of touch. Like the week one parent is traveling and the other one's at home, balancing everything just fine, until one kid gets strep, the other one lice... and then the gerbil looks very, very sick, and dies despite small animal urgent care. (Yes, they have special, very expensive treatments for parents whose kids beg, "Do something! We can't just let Butterball die!") Someone's work gets thwarted, again. Maybe you manage to give the kids what they need; maybe, just maybe, you get your work done. But your relationship? That takes a direct hit. Too many of these hits, and someone is likely to go nuclear... like that time you stayed up typing a three-page, single-spaced summary of what's going wrong and read it to your spouse upon his return from yet another business trip.

Something must be done, but beware the quick fix. It's been suggested that couples have a "weekly meeting" instead of date night to smooth over these rough times—updating each other on key issues such as his work and her concerns about the children. Does that sound sexy to you? Unless those conversations orient both people to actually *share in the work at home* and actively support mutual fulfillment in the external world, forget about it. It won't be effective, because it's not *affective*. It's just business professors reaching your home and bedroom to "professionalize" how you relate to each other, as they've done with everything else. We already know how that feels. Yuck.

WE ARE MAKING OURSELVES PHYSICALLY SICK

The stories we tell ourselves provide us with cognitive, intellectual permission to continue doing what we are doing—turning away from home in order to lean into work. When we move away from our children during the critical early years, we aren't only keeping ourselves from developing

89

empathy. We are also making ourselves sick. The problem is that when we swallow this guilt, it's not gone. It's still in there. Over time, it makes a lot of us feel sick. And we can't do empathy when we are sick. We can't really do anything when we are sick. Which brings us back to self-care. Remember, empathy is selfish first. Another important piece of empathic development is self-care.

Quantity time at the office gets in the way of empathy long before children come along because it gets in the way of our own self-care. So much of what we learn and do moves us further away from *taking care*, of even ourselves. Some of us work and travel so much that we write heartfelt goodbye notes to receptionists at hotels, where we feel more at home than in our apartment. We end up on more than a year's worth of antibiotics, unable to kick strep throat time and again for lack of sleep—all the while feeling conflicted about the human implications of some of the work we are doing. And increasingly, women especially resolve to never get married or have kids (or to put their eggs on ice) because there is no time to date.[98]

That's no way to live. We all know what to do: Eat well, exercise, do yoga, meditate, read good books, be with nature…and surround ourselves with good friends and family. But that's a lot to squeeze into the limited quality time we have away from work.

Oh, and then there is sleep. We're starting to remember something we knew when we were babies. Sleep matters. A lot. So much so that Arianna Huffington gave a TED talk and wrote a book about it—*The Sleep Revolution*. A whole book. About going to bed on time. Didn't we all read *Goodnight Moon*? How did we forget?! How is it that we can ignore the signals our bodies give us over days, weeks, and years of abysmal self-care? And why do we think we'll be able to kick those workaholic habits after this project, that job, or the big promotion? That's not how addiction works. Self-care is not automatic.

And once kids come along, finding time to care for ourselves only becomes more of a challenge. All the while, the stakes get higher because the kids are watching. And they've started to tell us that our lives don't look like much fun. They've started to wonder why growing up is even a good thing. Just ask. They'll tell you. "Do as I say, not as I do" doesn't fly anymore...if it ever did.

DECLINING BIRTHRATES:
THERE IS MORE THAN ONE WAY FOR THIS ALL TO END

Time has become such a problem that we aren't having children like we used to. Have you read the news lately? Women are not so interested in having babies. Our birthrate is at the lowest point in history, with 60 births to 1000 women last quarter.[99] This outcome is *despite* the fact that fertility treatments continue to improve. At the heart of this growing trend is the inability of women to envision working in today's world while raising a child. The two are incompatible. The refusal to have children is one very brave and logical solution for those who believe they do not have enough time to bring life into the world.

The anthology *Selfish, Shallow, and Self-Obsessed: Sixteen Writers on the Decision Not to Have Kids*, though far from a scientific survey, does shed some light on the reasons for these decisions.[100] Some contributors chose not to have children because they were enjoying their life as it was and didn't want to restrict their freedom. Others did not feel that they had the temperament, instinct, or mental stability for the job. One woman, who linked her own depression to her mother's long work absences, did not feel it would be fair to her child if she continued working. And she couldn't imagine giving up her job. Today, women in their thirties represent the first generation of grown children of women who participated in the workforce full swing. What is this decision telling us about how they experienced their own childhood in a home with a working mother?

In terms of continuing our species, this is a problem. It's a problem that statistics are bearing out. Taken to its natural conclusion, the decrease in procreation becomes a risk akin to climate change. There is more than one way for all of this to end.

But this is the price of progress, right? One generation makes sacrifices so the next can have a better life. For women especially, all of this hard work was meant to give us more of a voice. Let's see how it's going.

CHAPTER 12

Women Aren't Leading

Here is something else related to our empathy deficit disorder: More than 50 years after the feminist revolution, women are still not leading.

Not as much as we thought they would be by now. By and large, women are not leading in government. For the most part, they are not leading in corporate America. In the nonprofit and education worlds? Same story. More than 50 years after the feminist revolution, women hold a minority of leadership positions in all segments of the workforce. How do we know? Let's look at the facts:

Corporate America: As of the latest Catalyst report in 2015, women are 45% of the US labor force, but only ~19.2% of board seats, and ~4.6% of CEOs.

But maybe it's improving? Recently, not so much. The year 2015 was great for CEOs looking for new jobs, as long as you weren't a woman. Nearly 17% of the world's largest 2,500 public companies changed their CEOs, the highest turnover since PWC began tracking these numbers 16 years ago. But the trend for incoming women CEOs in the US and

Canada has been heading south for the last three years. Even with a few more additions in 2016, at this rate, gender parity in the C-suite will take 45 more years.[101]

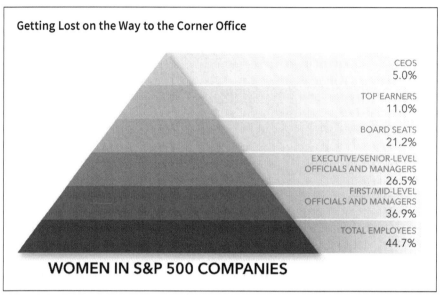

Getting Lost on the Way to the Corner Office

CEOS
5.0%

TOP EARNERS
11.0%

BOARD SEATS
21.2%

EXECUTIVE/SENIOR-LEVEL
OFFICIALS AND MANAGERS
26.5%

FIRST/MID-LEVEL
OFFICIALS AND MANAGERS
36.9%

TOTAL EMPLOYEES
44.7%

WOMEN IN S&P 500 COMPANIES

Government: Today, women comprise only 23% of Congress, despite the fact that we comprise 50% of the population. This means our government is representative only in name. Women fill only 22% of cabinet positions, and the lower-ranking ones at that.[102] How many US governors are women? Nine. Nine out of 50.[103] And the US has never had a woman president.

Nonprofits: While women hold the majority of nonprofit positions, men hold the majority of leadership positions. In large nonprofits, approximately 70% of leaders are male, as is the composition of their boards.[104] Enough said.

Share of Incoming Women CEOs, US & Canada, 2004–2015

Source: Strategy & https://www.strategyand.pwc.com/ceosuccess#Intro

Academia: Women in academia fare no better, even though they start strong. Women students comprise more than half of college students (57%) and half of all tenure-track faculty positions. Then, they get lost on the way to leadership, just as they do everywhere else. Women hold just 37.5% of tenured positions, 39% of dean positions, and 26% of college presidencies. Upon closer examination, the trade-offs get clearer. Married STEM chicks with children are 35% less likely than married men with children to get a tenure-track position after finishing their doctorate.[105]

Fifty years after the feminist revolution, and this is all we've got.

As of October 2016, global gender equity is moving even more slowly than before. The pace of change has become so painfully sluggish that researchers at the World Economic Forum (WEF) recently called it a "dramatic slowdown" that would mean—at current speeds—we won't get to equality for 170 years. In 2015, that timespan was 118 years. Change was gathering pace until 2013, the researchers said; but since then it's tailed off.[106]

But, hey, the US is a leader, right? Not by a long shot…and it's getting worse.

The most surprising finding was that the US has fallen far and fast in the rankings—to 45th place in 2016, from 23rd the previous year.

Why? "Women's labor-force participation has declined over the past year, and is 'stagnating among legislators,' senior officials and managers," according to the WEF.[107]

We're educated and chomping at the bit, though.

On the positive side, the WEF noted that the US has reached gender parity in education. Women in the country are as well educated as men, reflecting a global trend in which women in 95 countries now go to university in equal or higher numbers than men. However, parity in education combined with lack of it in the workplace creates its own problem: a large pool of qualified women whose skills are being underused and who are being poorly rewarded.[108]

WOMEN LEADERS IMPROVE THE BOTTOM LINE

All of this news comes in the midst of *mounting evidence* that women and diversity overall in leadership *actually improves* the bottom line. We are still doing these studies, and people continue to be surprised. That alone says something, doesn't it? Such studies correlating diversity and performance have been making news for at least the last decade.[109]

A recent report by Ernst and Young concluded that having at least 30% of women in leadership positions added 6% to net profit margins.[110] Maybe people don't understand or believe these data? Or maybe these studies are somehow beside the point? In any case, women go to work. But they don't lead. And the situation is getting worse.

So let's ask again: Who rises? Who isn't weighed down by the burden of close personal relationships? Who doesn't let guilt get in the way? Who's not busy working on their affective empathy? Who's got what it takes?

The psychopath. The badass. The queen bee.

But not hands-on parents, that's for sure. Not the people who are most in touch with that precious resource of the future—affective empathy. And because hands-on parents are still mostly women, it should be no surprise that women are still not leading.

CHAPTER 13

Solving the Fundamental Problem of Time

"Let's do the time warp again. It's a just a jump to the right..."
—*Rocky Horror Picture Show*

All of these changes in leadership and the economy hinge on something else—solving our time problem. Ensuring that parents have time at home with their babies and children to cultivate their asset class, their superpower of the future—affective empathy—is of primary importance. It all flows from how we spend time. How could the network help us with that?

There is a good chance that in the future, we will have a new way to work. Different aspects of our networked economy are likely to impact how we allocate time in the future.

ABUNDANCE

Peter Diamandis and Steven Kotler, among others, make it wonderfully clear that we are at a pivot point. We are nearing a time when everyone on earth could live without scarcity—food, water, shelter, etc.—within the next few decades. With no new technology. Maybe we have enough thingamajigs and whatchamacallits after all. Millennial behavior suggests that this may be the case. Today's young people are spending more time on social networks than on accumulating stuff. They are no longer hanging out at the mall.

So this is not a race to make more. It is now a matter of distribution and inclusion. It's a matter of finding the right problems to work on. That will be the new work. Do we need to try to live forever? Or should we focus on the abysmal rates of infant mortality in this country? Should we try to inhabit a new planet? Or should we try to make sure more of our earthly islands like Bangladesh don't go underwater? Should we make more ramen apps, or give people an extra half hour at home to cook dinner?

Who matters and how do they matter? The fact that nonprofits are growing revenue faster than GDP is a clue about the direction we are moving. Work for the public good is outpacing work aimed at maximizing profits.

Not only will this new kind of work rely on our skill of choice—affective empathy—but it will require less time. Can you see it? It is a different kind of work.

AUTOMATION

Automation is coming our way. Automation of physical labor is moving ahead, leaving a lot of people spitting mad about it.[111] Now, the cognitive activities that made geeks and smart people the top dogs of the knowledge economy are also being taken over by robots. What is left?

Well, there is still something robots can't do. They cannot speak for the emotional human experience that lies at our core. They can cognate but they can't feel. Because feeling resides in our limbic brain and is built through the experience of living. It comes from the narrative of our birth, the specter of death, and our most important relationships. There are no shortcuts to being uniquely human. The work that will remain is feeling work. This is why robots will never be able to rock our babies or care for our aging parents in the Alzheimer's unit. They may be able to remind them when it's time to eat and perhaps even feed patients in the advanced stages, but they can't relate emotionally. That's especially sad when advanced Alzheimer's patients, much like babies, have only their emotional brain for communicating with the outside world.

This kind of work also will save us time. Because in this case, affective empathy becomes both the work of home and the work of work. We get to spend all day long working on our affective empathy power.

ZERO MARGINAL COST

Finally, we need to talk about zero marginal cost. Just as John Maynard Keynes prophesied about capitalism nearly a century ago, "A point may soon be reached, much sooner perhaps than we are all of us aware of, when these needs are satisfied in the sense that we prefer to devote our further energies to non-economic purposes."[112] That time may almost be here.

We are quickly approaching the point at which it will cost nothing to produce an additional widget. That means more and more things will be free. And then what? Do we still need to go to work? This circles back to abundance. When we have enough and we no longer need to do physical or cognitive work to get it, what are we left with? We are left with time to tend to each other. So you see—we may have time after all.

And thank goodness for that. We will need that time. We will need that time so that we can grow our affective empathy. Because in this new world where the new work will be human, our affective empathy is all that we have. It is our tool, our skill, our currency. Affective empathy will be the new asset class. Our affective empathy will dictate our success and survival in this new world. It will help us see each other for who we really are. That was always the real work, wasn't it?

It is hard to predict how all of this will unfold and result in the time shift we so desperately need. But one thing we do know is that underlying all of these changes are some principles of physics that we need to share. At the core of the time shifts we are about to experience is the truism that empathy itself collapses time.

THE WRINKLE IN TIME IS EMPATHY

Empathy collapses time, effectively buying you more of your most scarce resource. Our friend Seung Chan Lim, a.k.a. "Slim," talks about empathy and efficiency. Check him out. He likes to do an exercise asking two people to face each other and say, "Tell me the truth" three times.

People who know each other get right down to it. People who don't know each other also arrive at some truth, but it takes until the third time. When was the last time someone told you the truth? When was the last time you felt safe enough to do so yourself? Don't we all need it? Wouldn't it save you time if you could cut to the chase? This is what empathy does. It saves you time by cutting to the chase. The upshot of Slim's message is that realizing empathy gets us more *efficiently* to *resonance* with other human beings and universal truth. And this is the stuff of which innovation is made.

So, here's the bottom line: If you practiced empathy, you'd get to innovation more quickly. And you would save time (= $) because empathy collapses time.

Speaking of time, articles abound exacting the efficiency of the working parent, but why is that... really? The opportunity cost of time has a clear, cute human face, so we waste less of it. Similarly, we don't abide nonsense. We also become very good at what looks like multitasking, but is really switching tasks very quickly, because it's hard for kids to wait. But we think there is something more, and it's related to empathy. We'll leave it to the social scientists to devise the experiments and write the papers, but you already know what we mean.

Ever work with a partner who finishes your sentences? Or played on a team that enters "the zone" of peak performance? Or been part of that rare project team that was actually GREAT at including everyone and coming up with answers no one person could have known? These are not linear processes, nor are they individual accomplishments. And they feel great too, don't they? That's because for a little while, you're suspended, outside of the most unifying and scarce resource of all: time. Rather than living and working side by side, putting one piece together and then the next, you're working together.

Madeleine L'Engle's *Wrinkle in Time* may have been science fiction, but for those of us who have been there and done that, she was also describing the divine experience of collapsing time via empathy. Check it out for yourself. See if empathy does that for you.

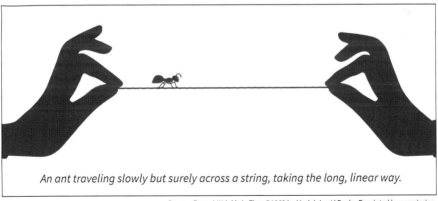

An ant traveling slowly but surely across a string, taking the long, linear way.

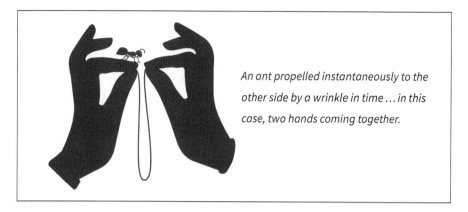

An ant propelled instantaneously to the other side by a wrinkle in time … in this case, two hands coming together.

But we are here now. A black hole devoid of empathy.

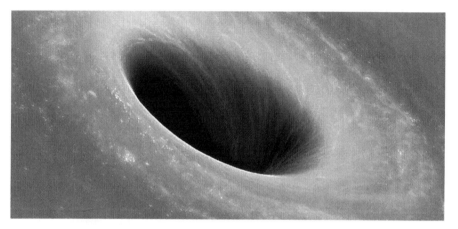

And we are time poor. Do we have to be?

TIME POVERTY

Let's start with the endless meetings in which nothing is done or decided, and everyone is checking their smartphones for a little dopamine hit to help them get by in relative emotional equanimity despite the Dilbert-esque nature of the whole scene. Next up, how about the mountains of emails threatening to bury you every day, with "cc" lava devouring every speck of time outside of said meetings. Then, there are the conference calls in which you [*fill in the blank*] instead of listen to the speaker.

Hot off the presses—multitasking is a myth, by the way. Now, layer on work cultures in which there is so much fear and distrust that whatever DOES get decided or done via meeting or email or text or conference call gets undone within a day or so...or comes up against such hard barriers that the whole project becomes an exercise in frustration, passing the buck, and managing expectations.

But maybe you're not in business. Maybe you work on a shop floor, in a doctor's office, a lawyer's office, or in front of a sixth-grade class. Productivity, efficiency, effectiveness...drive the need for one more gadget, patient, client, and school test topic. Time is money and there is never enough.

It was funny in the TV episode of I Love Lucy when Lucy and Ethel fell behind wrapping chocolates on the assembly line.[113] The job started out nicely and easily. Lucy, in pearls and lipstick, had it all under control. Then the conveyor belt started going faster and faster, and the chocolates went whizzing by. The ladies could not keep up. At first, we envied them popping some chocolates in their mouths as a stopgap. A deliciously sweet solution. Pretty soon, though, their cheeks were loaded, as were their pockets and hats. Funny but messy. That was 1952. No one is laughing anymore.

And we're apprenticing our children in this art. Since the workday is longer than the school day, our kids have been scheduled for second and third shifts as well. Enrichment, we call it. But they're tired, too. They're time poor.

All of this for what? What if we just...stopped?

What if we just stopped the roller coaster? Would we still have enough stuff? We think so. What if we cut the workday in half? Took half the meetings off the calendar? Stopped sending emails that don't matter? Picked up the phone to solve a debate within minutes instead? What if we designed school around what helps kids' brains grow and work around what will create an abundant world for everyone?

It's crazy.

Or maybe it's not. Have you noticed? Things are changing. Beacons of hope are emerging:

- Amazon is now trying a 30-hour workweek for a technical team, including managers, so flextime doesn't mean left behind anymore.

- Development experts are talking about a 20-hour workweek. No kidding.

- Mexico's richest man is proposing a three-day workweek. For everyone. Not just the rich.

- A lot of people are asking, "Isn't it time to kill the 9-to-5 schedule?"

- Bloomberg, the financial company, offers all parents 20 weeks of paid leave as the battle for employees in a tight labor market grows.

- Research is finding that 39 is the magic number of hours we should work per week.[114] More than that and it negatively affects our mental health.

So what's the next phase of this time/work warp? There are lots of futurists, economists, and politicians debating this very question. We don't pretend to have all the answers, but maybe this question helps: *How do we get from where we are now to that dream of co-creation at home, with meaningful work wrapped around it?*

At the highest level, the answer will include:

- Using automation to free up time for more creative and caring work for everyone

- Valuing caring work differently than we do today

- Creating financial tools and policies that support both of the above

There has been talk already of programming the necessary specifics (e.g., universal base income [UBI], parental leave). Maybe the context is what we're lacking. And it's not so crazy; just ask Finland, which has rolled out a pilot program that guarantees UBI for its lowest-income citizens.[115]

Maybe the time has come when we can all be human again.

But first, we need to stop leaving men out in the cold.

Clearing Up Our Mix-Ups about Sex, the Font of -Isms

CHAPTER 14

Mix-Up No. 3
The Biggest Mix-Up of All:
Caring Is Women's Work

For women (and some men) who have been struggling to make untenable work-home paradigms work, the changing landscape gives us hope. To think we may be witnessing the birth of a new economic system where empathy is the new asset class is exciting. The possibility that empathic leaders will be in demand and that our work will have more soul is heartening. As is the prospect of having more time to grow our affective empathy. But we have two remaining problems:

1. What about the nightmare at home? Absent changes to home life, a path forward for women in "leadership" seems unlikely.

2. What about our men? They are not known for their affective empathy. It hurts us to think that they may be left behind. Because we love them.

Fortunately, here we can kill two birds with one stone. The answer to both of our remaining problems is the same:

It's time to bring the men home.

This brings us to another mix-up—perhaps the biggest, most damaging mix-up of all: that *caring* is women's work. Caring is not something real men can truly spend time doing, especially any serious executive. It's hard to play in the big leagues with a papoose strapped on your back.

This is not a new mix-up. Women rather than men have been primary caretakers of children since the beginning of time in almost every known culture. Today, in the US and some parts of the world, things seem to be changing.[116] In our interviews with Millennial dads, we find that there is a greater willingness to share parenting responsibilities.

But this mix-up is still deeply ingrained in our culture. It may not be politically correct to admit it out loud, but we all know that most people *still* think that caring is women's work. It shows up in the statistics: Women provide the vast majority of hands-on caring for children as well as spouses, parents, parents-in-law, friends, and neighbors. This statistic is the same for paid and unpaid caregiving work.[117] When it comes to early childhood, these numbers are even larger.

Think of the way movies make us chuckle when they parody caring men. Male nurse Greg Focker is our favorite. Remember how hard we laughed when Ben Stiller's character in the 2000 movie, *Meet the Parents*, revealed his pink-collar profession to his incredulous and über-macho father-in-law-to-be (played to a T by Robert De Niro)?

While men and women *do* have different biology, there is nothing inherent in men's biology that makes them incapable of caring. Yet, the biology of gender is frequently invoked as a reason that men cannot be caretakers, despite the fact that the scientists who have taken a good hard look at this assumption have turned it on its head.

Sarah Blaffer Hrdy is one such scientist who has spent her career studying caretaking through an anthropological lens. As Hrdy explains, it is the interaction between biology and environment that matters for caretaking. To Hrdy, it makes no sense to discuss one without the other:

> *Instead of old dichotomies about nature versus nurture, attention needs to be focused on the complicated interactions among genes, tissue, glands, past experiences and environmental cues, including sensory cues provided by infants themselves and by other individuals in the vicinity. Complex behavior like nurturing, especially when tied to even more complex emotions like "love," are never genetically predetermined or environmentally produced.*[118]

So do men have what it takes to care? Hrdy concludes:

> *Rather than some magical "essence of mother," what makes a mother maternal is that she is (invariably)* **at the scene, hormonally primed, sensitive to infant signals, and related to the baby.** *These factors lower her threshold for giving of herself to satisfy the infant's needs. Once her milk comes in, the mother's urge to nurture grows stronger still .... These factors make the mother the likeliest candidate to become the primary caretaker.* **But they do not constitute an unyielding prescription.**[119]

WHAT IT TAKES TO CARE FOR A CHILD

So let's unpack Hrdy's observations to better assess whether men can care too. Caring for a child requires:

- **Being related.** According to current legal definitions, a parent may be related to a child through biology, adoption, marriage, or partnership. Being related is equal opportunity—same for moms and dads.

- **Being there.** Can men be physically present at the birth of their child and after that? We can't see why not. As long as work doesn't get in the way. Back when men had to go hunting to keep their families alive, perhaps it wasn't so possible. But times have changed, and being there physically with your child is more of a choice than it has ever been. For women AND men.

- **Being hormonally primed.** Women are perhaps more hormonally primed than men because of pregnancy and lactation. But new data is showing that if men are there in the room spending time with their baby, they become hormonally primed, too. We talked about this in Chapter 9, but it bears repeating.

When men engage in hands-on caring, something special happens. In *The Mommy Brain*, Katherine Ellison writes:

> The fatherly drug trip continues and in some ways intensifies once the new baby leaves the womb. At that point the levels of a man's testosterone—that intrinsically male hormone linked with competition and sexual and physical aggression—plummets by as much as one-third.[120]

(Don't worry fellas; it's not as bad as it sounds.) She continues, "Over the course of human history, this change probably helped calm men down and made them less likely to stray at the time their mates most need them."[121] She goes on to summarize more research, which shows other hormonal fluctuations in dads who care for their kids. Prolactin, oxytocin, and vasopressin all seem to play a role. Further, Ellison presents the conclusion reached by Harvard researchers: "If fathers begin to spend more time in childcare, one might expect the…gains for the men to be more like those we have obtained for women."[122]

The gains that the Harvard researchers are talking about have to do with affective empathy. And affective empathy is what it takes to read infant cues. The babies aren't talking yet, so our cognitive capacities aren't that useful. What they need from us is emotional and unconscious. Do women on the whole have more affective empathy than men to begin with? Perhaps. But men's affective empathy is by no means absent. And even if men do come to the table with less affective empathy, the fatherly drug trip associated with committing to their baby surely must help. Affective empathy is something that continues to grow for men and women alike, commensurate with the more time they spend caring for their baby.

Think about the men you know. Can you imagine them with a baby they love? When that baby smiles, do they smile back? When the baby cries, does it bother them enough that they notice? Probably, especially if it's their kid. Responding to a baby is not rocket science. We all have that capacity, since we were all babies once on the receiving end of that empathy. And *pssst*—here's a secret. Moms don't know what they are doing either after that baby is born. They figure it out as they hang around and get to know their baby. The baby teaches them, because empathy is a two-way street. When the poet Wordsworth wrote, "The Child is father of the Man," he was really onto something.

So back to our caring-requirement checklist. Hormonally primed? Women—check. Men—check. Able to read infant cues? Women—check. Men—check.

The Torah/Old Testament had a definitive test as well. Remember Solomon? First Kings 3:16–28 tells the story of two women who came to Solomon in a quandary. Each one claimed to be the mother of the same infant son. To resolve the dilemma, Solomon declared that he would cut the infant in half with his sword, giving half of the child to each mother. One mother agreed to Solomon's plan. The other woman begged him not to kill the baby but to give it to the other mother. And this is how

Solomon knew who the real mother was.

Perhaps it's that simple. If you would give up everything to save your child's life, you probably have exactly what it takes to care for your kid. And gender has nothing to do with that.

It appears that even when it comes to the biology of caring, men and women are more similar than we thought. Yet, somehow, we are still mixed up, believing that caring is women's work. This mix-up is costing men dearly. We are depriving men of the empathy development that will allow them agency in our new economy.

CHAPTER 15

Psychopaths Are People Too... Usually Men

We like to get mad at the corporate psychopath. We like to blame him for the way he exploits people for personal gain. We wonder how his conscience, his voice inside, lets him do things that wreak enormous collateral damage. But maybe he is a victim, too—of a system producing exactly what we would expect.

Many people with empathy deficits are a product of their environment. These are people who may have started out one way but were encouraged to lean out of their empathy by a system that rewarded "survival of the fittest" and marginalized the empathy they learned when mommy and daddy first gazed adoringly into their eyes. The lack of empathy is situational, triggered by circumstances. In fact, most of us feel situational zero empathy from time to time—which means what it sounds like. No empathy, no regrets, no remorse. Have you ever done something you regretted? Have you ever stepped on someone even just for the sake of efficiency? Yeah. We have too.

Evolutionary data support this. According to primatologist Dr. Frans de Waal, most people "lack a killer instinct." While war involves a whole lotta killing, this killing is not driven by widespread killer instincts. "Only a small percentage of men—perhaps 1 to 2 percent—does the vast majority of killing during a war.... Warfare is psychologically complex, and seems more a product of hierarchy and following orders than of aggression and lack of mercy."[123]

When we tease out the who's who in war, we see that being complicit doesn't mean that one's empathy has been erased. Usually it's just been shoved away, deep down inside our bodies and away from our cognitive brains. It usually emerges again after the war is over, in the form of PTSD, when, in the quiet of their suburban American homes, soldiers are forced to come to terms with the horror of what they just participated in.

Between 2% and 17% of American soldiers are diagnosed with PTSD.[124] It is responsible at alarming rates for morbidity and mortality once soldiers get home. But perhaps PTSD is less a disease and more a dis-ease. Maybe PTSD is really our healthy affective empathy screaming out in pain in hopes that someone will hear it. The psychopath's blood pressure remains steady when he kills. But men who are forced to kill and oppose their inner affective empathy feel regret, remorse, and guilt. They get sick, because the killing of other human beings goes against the way they are built.

Maybe the real psychopaths here are the cognitive psychologists who offer anti-PTSD training to soldiers before battle.[125] It's just not obvious how to eliminate PTSD without attempting to wipe out a person's conscience. The good news for us—and all mankind—is that our conscience cannot be exorcised away, any more than empathy training can make it grow where none exists.

Our conscience cannot be rebuked or silenced. It persists.

Evolutionary biology also shows us the role that the workplace can play in decreasing a person's empathy. Consider this. According to de Waal, primatologists have observed three ways to eliminate kindness in chimps, namely:

- pair them with strangers,
- put a panel between them so the other is out of sight, or
- give the partner a superior reward.[126]

And so what do we do at the office? We:

- demand quantity time with coworkers, away from family,
- put people in cubicles separated by partitions, and
- compete/top-grade employees in a man-made war for talent.

What are we doing to ourselves? Everyone is paying a price, but it's time to admit that in some ways, men have it worse.

MEN—DEPRIVED OR DEPRAVED?

It is hard to miss that men commit more crimes.[127]

- Males constituted 98.0% of those arrested for forcible rape.
- Males constituted 89.0% of those arrested for robbery.
- Males constituted 85.0% of those arrested for burglary.
- Males constituted 83.0% of those arrested for arson.
- Males constituted 81.5% of those arrested for motor vehicle theft.
- Males constituted 81.7% of those arrested for stolen property.
- Males constituted 81.7% of those arrested for vandalism.
- Males constituted 79.7% of those arrested for offenses against family and children.
- Males constituted 77.8% of those arrested for aggravated assault.
- Men are also diagnosed with empathy deficit psychiatric disorders at much higher rates than women.

Of the three zero-empathy personality disorders—psychopathy, narcissism, and borderline personality disorder—men outnumber women two to one.[128]

Why?

If empathy is the new asset class, and we don't want men to fall behind, this question must be answered. Is there some job that women do but men still don't do, even in this age of equal opportunity, that affects empathy?

The answer is yes. As we discussed earlier, women have more affective empathy because of the hands-on caring that they have done and continue to do almost exclusively. Women are overwhelmingly the ones feeding, holding, gazing at, rocking, and changing babies. Not men. Women are the ones that put the time into this job before the child is talking. Men come in later.

All of this caring has changed our DNA to enable our biological proclivity toward empathy. And it explains the rise in empathy that occurs in women over a lifetime—something that is not matched by men.[129]

WHEN ONLY WOMEN MOTHER, BOYS SUFFER

What happens when only women mother? Feminist theorists have been asking this question for decades. And it's a good one. Recent evolutionary and neuroscientific inquiry has given us data that illuminate some aspects of this question. But still, it is a difficult question to answer, because the experiment has never been done. Even today, few fathers are involved in early hands-on caring. Without a large enough sample size for our control group of fathers, we are unable to draw meaningful conclusions.

Enter Nancy Chodorow. In her groundbreaking 1979 book, *The Reproduction of Mothering*, Chodorow uses psychoanalytic theory to argue that many of the gender differences we attribute to biology or even socialization are actually the result of the asymmetrical structure of parenting. Girls are raised by women. Boys are not raised by men. Can you see where this is going?

Recognizing that we live in a gendered world, Chodorow suggests that girls readily identify with the nurturing role they associate with their mothers because moms see their girls as they see themselves. Because moms are already gendered, they cannot see their boys as they see themselves. The mirror is skewed. Boys must differentiate, setting the stage for more competitive drives.

Chodorow isn't talking about mere modeling. She is talking about something that takes place earlier and that is more fundamental, almost indiscernible from our genetic makeup. She is talking about the way that our parenting arrangements shape our earliest identity and thus, our relationship to the world. She is talking about a gendered sense of ourselves that is imprinted early and deeply, before our cognitive brain has time to sort things out. She is talking about a sense of belonging and connection that boys grow up missing because their dads aren't there when it matters most.

And so the gendered world our children are born into continues to be reproduced by women who mother girls, and women who mother boys, and men who mother no one. And men are losing out big-time.

＊

CHAPTER 16

When Only Women Care,
Men Are Underemployed

Today, the imprint of the male competitive drive is all around us. Our economic system is based on competition, our leadership structures are hierarchical, time is at the mercy of efficiency, and we collectively subscribe to the gospel of survival of the fittest. These models dominate. But the world is changing. We are questioning the fundamental assumptions about how we should set up our society and view the world. Because a lot of things are no longer working like they used to.

To review: Hierarchical leadership remains, but it isn't serving our men. Their companies aren't innovating or growing. And men aren't sure what has hit them. The guy they remember and want to emulate—the serious, solitary leader who put work first and told his underlings, "It's my way or the highway"—can no longer get things done. It's confusing, as is the prospect of a world without those pointy pyramids.

The factory jobs are going, going, gone. Manufacturing with its hard work, time clocks, and full employment are becoming a thing of the past. Through the "art of the deal," we may stall the inevitable for a little while, but those things are not coming back. First outsourcing, then automation. This very foundation of our economy, way of life, and way of working is changing.

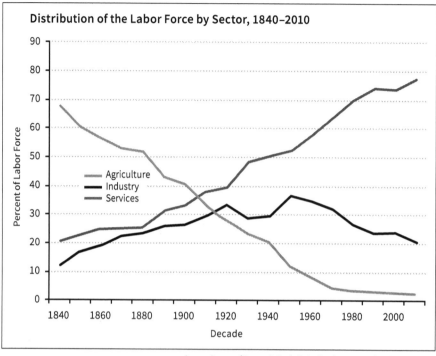

Distribution of the Labor Force by Sector, 1840–2010

Source: Bureau of Economic Analysis, National Income and Product Accounts
From Louis D. Johnson, "History Lessons: Understanding the Decline in Manufacturing," MinnPost, Feb. 2, 2012. Copyright © MinnPost.com, 2012. Reprinted with permission.

These changes feel new, but they've really been in the works for 100 years, shifting us from an agrarian to an industrial to a services economy in that timeframe.

The changes are not just affecting manual labor; computers are rapidly learning to do some white-collar and service-sector work, too. Existing technology could automate 45% of activities people are paid to do, according to a July 2016 report by McKinsey. These changes are destabilizing to the male identity. It used to be that a man's home was his castle and his work was never done. If all of this ground is shifting, what's a man to do?

Work that requires creativity, management of people, or caregiving is least at risk. But pink-collar (caregiving) jobs have historically been repulsive to men. That's too bad. In some parts of the country where manufacturing jobs have disappeared, caregiving jobs are in abundance and paying well. Yet men would rather be unemployed than take on these feminine jobs.[130] That shouldn't be surprising. When only women mother, men are forced to define themselves in opposition to the pink work that gave them life— if they want to be a man like dad. Millennial men, however, seem to be more open to caring work like nursing. Time will tell.

Isn't it interesting that women don't have the same aversion to male jobs? They are more like badges of honor. We know. We wore them. Also, let's face it: Traditionally male jobs have been more highly valued in our culture for a long time. How do we know? They pay more. But it's more than that. Because we are mothered by someone of our own gender, our gender identity is more fluid. We don't have to cling to it so desperately. We aren't threatened or punished for playing other roles. We have the template of that early relationship keeping us anchored inside.

*

CHAPTER 17

When Only Women Care, Men Die

Let's really think about this mix-up about caring being women's work. What would the world look like if more men did more caring? What would our little boys learn if daddies had more chances to rock them to sleep, pick them up from the bus, or be the kind of soccer coach who cares more about the *kids* than winning? What would our little boys act like if they modeled men who had more time to listen, hug, and play? Would we have as many wars? Would ISIS have as many willing recruits?

We know that 80% of violent crime is committed by men, not women. But why? Perhaps it is because men do not have as many chances to care. What about those fortunate girls who grow up under the care of dads who are there to wipe their noses when they are sick or to console them when their best friend breaks their heart? That's good juice for life. The kind that helps you know it when a great life partner comes along. For boys and girls alike, *true empathy from dad* is the real currency of the *actually* lucky sperm club.

The news is grim. This lack of belonging and connection is killing our men.

For the first time in 2015, a study in the *Proceedings of the National Academy of Sciences* found that mortality rates for middle-aged white American men are increasing, while rates for the rest of the world are plummeting. The reason given? An increase in "despair deaths."[131] Yes, it's as awful as it sounds. The reason more men are dying is because they are literally killing themselves with suicides, drugs, and alcohol. Men are in pain—deep psychic pain. Why?

Most agree that the loss of jobs in the manufacturing industry that occurred at the turn of this century has hit men hard. We have taken from men the reliable paycheck and their earning potential. In economic terms, this means that men can no longer afford goods and services that they once could afford and still need today. And they are unable to bounce back, because we never gave them the skills and education to adapt to the new technological economy.

But what else have we not given men? Is there another reason that they are unable to bounce back? Perhaps these men are dealing with a kind of emotional scarcity that is far more pernicious.

What are these health trends trying to tell us? What do we see when we really look instead of looking away? Maybe "real men" are even tougher than they used to be. Let's review a few American icons.

John Wayne's got nothin' on them. His movie characters were quintessential cowboys. Tough. Strong. The men wanted to be him, and the women wanted to be with him. But his characters also had prominent worry lines on their foreheads. John Wayne admitted what everyone knows: "All battles are fought by scared men who'd rather be someplace else."[132]

It might worry him that today's "real men" are taught from a young age not to admit vulnerability; they get angry and drink instead. Today's real men don't rely on others for emotional support; but heroin is cheap. Today's real men are providers. Until they aren't. Can't. When the self-loathing of the loss of this identity becomes too great, they check out and hope insurance covers the rest.

Let's check in with some other popular culture male archetypes.

Clint Eastwood's early characters were tough guys. Dirty Harry was an icon. Generations of men (and women) loved repeating, "Go ahead, make my day"—even if they weren't squinting in the sun, finger on the trigger of a gun pointed at the bad guy. Clint is 87 now. Maybe he wonders what the hell has happened to men in this country since he gave them Dirty Harry to emulate.

Archie Bunker ushered in a whole new era for the modern American patriarch. He was the dad of *All in the Family*, which figured prominently on American TVs in the 1970s. With his big gut and even bigger mouth, there was Archie, holding forth on everything and everyone from his comfy chair near the TV in the living room. He was trying to make sense of cultural changes afoot in his home and the world at large. Archie always had answers, but he was frustrated that the world seemed to move without him. Actually, he was angry most of the time. He looked like a heart attack waiting to happen.

Or was it actually fear? Yeah, if we looked carefully into his eyes, we could see it was really fear. That's the root of anger, after all. And there is a lot to be afraid of. Like, for example, fighting in a battle when you'd rather be someplace else...or becoming a minority and dying too young.

It is no surprise that a more recent study by the CDC suggests that increases in heart disease, diabetes, and respiratory disease are also on the rise for these men. These diseases account for another portion of this growing trend in mortality. While not considered despair deaths, it is not such a stretch to see them as similarly related to stress and despair. According to *Mommy Brain*, we know that "High testosterone increases harmful cholesterol, raising a man's chances of heart disease and stroke."[133] We also know that when a man spends time with his kids, his testosterone plummets by one third. You have to wonder whether men's bodies are trying to tell them something. You have to wonder if too much time not caring is costing men their lives.

Why DO women live longer than men, anyway? Why do we accept this fact as an immutable function of sex rather than a pernicious kind of counterintuitive discrimination? Even though historically, medical research has focused almost exclusively on white men. Seriously. What's up, Doc? Is it possible that even as our kids give us gray hairs, they are staving off disease and prolonging our lives just by being in our care?

Go give your kids two hugs and call us in the morning.

CHAPTER 18

When Only Women Care, Boys Yearn and Sexism Ferments

What else in our world might change if men did more caring? Might we have less sexism? From casual fat-shaming comments, to deliberate actions that keep women out of the corner office, to the human trafficking of girls right here in our backyard, it's a problem. And it's not getting better as quickly as we would like.

The sexism on display during the 2016 US Presidential campaign was breathtaking. We have tried things, such as encouraging girls to code rather than play with dolls, and chiding women when they get the coffee at the office. To men, we give sensitivity training. When that fails, we try muzzling and shaming them with political correctness, forcing them to publicly proclaim ideas that in private they don't believe. Have you noticed how relieved some of them are to have those shackles removed by "leaders" who rely on divisiveness and vulgarity to rally support? Right. Muzzling doesn't work. So, more than 50 years after women threw off the yoke of home and began the mass exodus to work, even occasionally becoming The Boss, sexism prevails. Men are still dominating and denigrating women as if their lives depend on it.

Clearly, we are missing something. What haven't we tried?

Maybe we would not have as much sexism if men did more of the caring of children. Would that work? It is the one thing, after all, that we have not tried. *We have not done that experiment.* By and large, women on average have been the primary caretakers of children, especially young children, across time and space. So back to more theory. Try this and see if it makes sense.

Sexism is learned through experience, within relationships, like anything else. It is planted most firmly in the early years. As a result, it is largely unconscious and often irrational. Gender stereotypes are planted the day kids are born and are cared for by a mother rather than a father. Was that true for you? Chances are it was. Still today, women in the US spend on average twice as much time caring for their children as men do.[134] When it comes to early childhood, this discrepancy is largest from birth to age three.

So what happens? In the best scenario with a loving and present mom, very young children become attached. They depend on her. They love her like no other. She is everything. This is not irrational. Mom feeds, bathes, clothes, comforts. She does for. Then she does with. Then she stands by to admire, as kids learn to do for themselves, and come to realize their separate identities.[135]

For girls, this is not so much of a problem. Lucky for them, girls share something very fundamental with mom—a gender. So their sense of connection with all that they know and all that they love remains unthreatened in this particular way. From the perspective of gender, they can ultimately separate from mom with a sense that they still have all they need to feel loved, safe, and secure.

But boys can have it kinda tough if dad is not prominent in their caring world. Boys must accept that they are different from mom in a fundamental way. They must accept that they are not mom, gender-wise. And that's a lot to contend with when you are a helpless little boy whose life depends on mom. Mom is the best thing that ever happened to you. Mom is the apple of your eye. But from the perspective of gender, you can never fully be her or even be like her. This identity chasm can be a tough crossing for boys. Some have observed that it gives rise to conflict, resentment, and rage.[136] It gives rise to a rage against the opposite sex that never goes away. Can you see it? Maybe in your coworker, neighbor … or nocturnal, tweeting politicians?

Even if feminist psychology is not your thing, perhaps you can see there is something to it. At the very least, we would be naïve *not* to expect that something very different happens for girls than happens for boys when their first and most important relationship is so predominantly with a woman.

And maybe you believe "gender identity" is our hang-up, not the kids'. You're probably right, but our hang-ups get passed on along with experiences and our genes, don't they? Sure, kids don't necessarily intuitively know their gender from the get-go. Remember that awesome scene in the movie *Free to Be You and Me* where boy meets girl in the hospital nursery, but they don't know who's what?! Right. It's like that. The idea that we are boys or girls (or even something in between) emerges as a discovery over time.

Kids take their cue from the way parents treat them. So because of our deep-seated gender identity, we experience boys differently from girls, even when they are babies. The trucks or dolls are how kids act out this underlying relational identity that is established before kids even have words. It's not good or bad. It just is.

So, it's hard for a boy not to feel a little dissed when dad is not around. Some boys manage beautifully; but why should we leave the rest with so much emotional work? Here is more from Nancy Chodorow.[137]

- Girls are more relational because they can more fully identify with the one that is holding them, caressing them, feeding them, changing them, and talking to them on a regular basis. Boys cannot fully identify, because their gender puts them in the metaphorical out-group. Hierarchy becomes a coping mechanism for dealing with that loss, as does competition. Reminder: The new economy depends on win-win. Maybe dads should step in.

- Girls are uninhibited to be dependent while boys are fiercely independent. Mother and child rely on each other. Children depend on their mothers for physical and psychic life. Moms who are healthy also depend on their children. Their well-being is tied up in the well-being of their children. Not in a fused way, but in a healthy kind of mutuality. But when boys come to terms with the fact that they cannot internalize the feminine ideal of mom, it's a loss. They have to go it alone. And have to use power tools to externally control what they can't internalize within. Reminder: The new economy depends on the mutuality of relationships, not power tools. Dads, time to step up to the plate.

- Girls are empathic. Boys are less so. When mom and you are engaged in a dance of co-creation, empathy is everywhere. *But boys who do not see men doing empathy think letting go of empathy is part of what it takes to become a man.* And they really want to grow up to be men. We just sigh and say, "Boys will be boys." It's a shame. Because we know that empathy is the currency of the new economy. Dads, we need you. Please come.

As kids grow in their cognitive abilities, they take up our narratives as well. Sometimes, these narratives are loaded with hierarchies based on birth order and gender. Parents aren't the only ones infusing kids' cognitive narratives about who's in, who's out, who's above, and who's below. The culture surrounding a family is filled with stories, too. It's a lot for kids to process, profoundly affecting how they see the world and live out their place in it. Very often, gendered narratives leave little room for boys to grow with their feelings intact and girls to realize their power. Venus and Mars are of our own making.

Fred Rogers showed a better way. He cared for children before it was cool for men to go there. The sweater. The sneakers. He was decidedly un-cool. But he was ahead of his time, publicly channeling something universally true but countercultural.  His testimony in support of Public Television in 1969 gave Senator John O. Pastore, Chairman of the Subcommittee on Communications, goose bumps.[138] Imagine that! Senator Pastore said so in public—in front of his fellow lawmakers. It was unexpected.

Fred Rogers's six-minute Senate speech finished with this song, acknowledging the internal, emotional lives of boys and girls and all of us...even senators, then and now:

*

What Do You Do with the Mad That You Feel? (Song)[139]

What do you do with the mad that you feel
When you feel so mad you could bite?
When the whole wide world seems oh, so wrong...
And nothing you do seems very right?

What do you do? Do you punch a bag?
Do you pound some clay or some dough?
Do you round up friends for a game of tag?
Or see how fast you go?

It's great to be able to stop
When you've planned a thing that's wrong,
And be able to do something else instead
And think this song:

I can stop when I want to
Can stop when I wish
I can stop, stop, stop any time.
And what a good feeling to feel like this
And know that the feeling is really mine.
Know that there's something deep inside
That helps us become what we can.
For a girl can be someday a woman
And a boy can be someday a man.

CHAPTER 19

When Only Women Care,
All the -Isms Ferment

If empathy can help solve sexism, maybe it can help with other -isms as well. It makes sense, doesn't it? With healthy affective empathic circuitry and cognitive stories that include all people—even all living beings—others' pain is intolerable, and joy multiplies across the entire planet.

MENTAL HEALTH DEPENDS ON EMPATHY

Cyndi Dale, author of *The Spiritual Power of Empathy*, suggests these issues are indeed related:

> The reality is that "distorted empathy" can create the conditions for many "isms," including personality disorders (i.e. borderline, narcissism, and more); psychiatric issues (bipolar, schizophrenia, and more); and specific challenges in regard to Post-Traumatic Stress Syndrome, ADHD, autism spectrum disorders, depression, anxiety, and addictions. And if you are like me, it can make you vulnerable and susceptible to relationships with people with one or more "isms," and ultimately finding yourself taking care of problems that aren't your own.[140]

Maybe empathic consciousness development is a new way to look at mental health, from the inside out. As reading is to intellectual development, healthy affective empathy is to emotional stability and relationships.

And it is through relationships that our identity emerges. First with family (vertical), and then also with friends/colleagues/fellows (horizontal). Sometimes children fall "far from the tree" through a combination of biological and environmental factors; Andrew Solomon wrote a phenomenal book of the same name, in which parental empathy with children who have different identities (e.g., deaf, autistic) is healing for families.[141] And relating to people who are different from us—whether they are our parent, a sibling, a coworker, or a bitter political rival—is central in our race toward global consciousness.

So, the more practice we get in our family, the more natural it is to stretch our affective empathy to people who are different. Then the stories we hear in our family, our schools, and our communities (local, national, global) create the cognitive stories about who's in, who's out, why, and what that means—in other words, the foundation for our cognitive empathy.

THE ROOTS OF RACISM

All of the -isms (racism, sexism, genderism, ageism...you-name-it-ism) are the bitter fruit of the tree of patriarchy, with deep roots in the most foundational and degenerative human mix-up of all: hierarchy. It's as old as time for humans to stratify each other (and other sentient beings, like the ones we eat) in a way that creates winners and losers (who suffer and too often die). If you are at the top of the heap (or, you could say, sitting atop the biggest pointy pyramid of all), the rest of the world is supposedly for your use, whether to satisfy your desires, bear your children, cook your meals, build your Egyptian pyramid, pick your cotton in Alabama, or work in your factories in Detroit for minimum wage.

Why do we stratify each other? Is it innately human? Is it "in our genes" and unavoidable? Or is it something we learned over time that can be unlearned? In times of scarcity and deprivation, competition can be fierce, so fierce that we forget to help each other survive. We forget our evolutionary glue is empathy. But now, we live in one of the richest countries on earth at a time of relative abundance. We might expect the –isms to fall away. They are not. At all.

Racism, sexism, and all of the other –isms are alive and kicking, hard. The presidential election of 2016 and its aftermath have been especially revealing. We're fighting in the usual ways but not getting anywhere new; in fact, the powers that be seem to be retrenching, branding threats to the patriarchy as "fake news." Patriarchy still feels crucial for survival. That's because emotional scarcity remains, even when physical scarcity could be a thing of the past.

The national hierarchy is already becoming upended; for example, among US children, minorities will be the majority by 2020.[142] In a representative democracy where votes carry weight, which translates into political power, that shift is huge. People feel it. What will white men have left if they don't have the usual trifecta of power tools: political, financial, physical? (The National Rifle Association brings all three together beautifully—or in an ugly way, depending on your view.) Have powerful white men lost touch with their humanity up there at the top of the national pointy pyramid? They've been boxed out of their human superpower of affective empathy. Of course, they are going to fight to retain the usual sources of power, until they see there is something more.

Things are changing quickly. It's confusing and scary for many people, but it's also encouraging. Physical abundance is possible, for the first time, globally. Win-lose is giving way to win-win as the way to succeed in the future. And our fear of the other is dissipating as we get to know him and see he is us—with the same hopes, dreams, and desires as any Homo sapiens through the ages. To be loved. To belong. To survive with minimum pain and optimal joy. People are waking up to something beyond patriarchy. Something better for everyone, including the patriarchs who seem to have it all yet are so miserable. Our global connectivity, though far from perfect, does help us see each other more clearly. It helps us see "the other" is us.

The immigrants of today are our great-grandparents, time-shifted. Black or white, LGBT, man or woman…deep inside we're all the same. And few common experiences have the power to bind us more clearly—to supersede cultural stories about in-group and out-group—than how we all feel about our children. We see inspirational examples every day. How about the Israeli and Palestinian parents who lost children, coming together for peace? Or the 200 Klansmen who gave up their robes to Daryl Davis, a Black man who has been befriending members of the Ku Klux Klan for 30 years. There are few more impressive examples of out-group empathy, a skill he honed moving around the globe with his parents who were in the Foreign Service during most of his early childhood.[143]

And that work has legs. Because the more we can see ourselves in others who are not like us, the more opportunity we have to exercise our empathy muscles. The more supported and better we parent, the more likely our children get what they need to develop healthy affective and cognitive empathy in the first place. Then the virtuous cycle takes over; relationships expand to include so many others until there is no "other" anymore. There is just us. What a wonderful world that would be.

WHAT'S DAD GOT TO DO WITH IT?

We're not nearly there yet. Even where physical abundance is a real possibility and cognitive abundance is well on its way, emotional scarcity reigns, especially for boys and men. That's a real and raw deal—an embodied experience which then affects our relationships with each other and our impact on the physical world.

It is clear. We need men to be dads. We need them to care. We need it for our boys. We need it for our men—the men of today, and the men of the future. What's holding us back? What are we missing? What will it take to get rid of this mix-up? What if we made it easier for men to be home with their kids?

Maybe men have been playing the wrong game all along...and losing at the one that matters most: growing their hearts. Ouch. That hurts. But it's time we admit how complicit we *all* are in this game. We need to stop boxing men out of their chances to grow empathy.

Because somehow, the sexes don't seem to be fighting over this particular job. Women have fought men for a place in virtually every other profession, with men in turn fighting back to salvage their place. Not when it comes to childcare, however. Childcare has been the booby prize of the last 50 years especially. Instead of fighting for that privilege, we've been passing it off to our lowest-paid workers. In the process, we take these workers away from their own children so that they can make enough money to put their children in cheap(er) daycare. "Leaning in" is really leaning on others to raise your kids.[144] Now *that's* mixed up.

And even if men wanted to claim the childcare, society makes it hard. Besides the financial pressures that we all have to work full throttle, men still have even more social pressure. Social pressure NOT to take paternity leave. Social pressure NOT to be a stay-at-home dad. Social pressure NOT to be vulnerable. Real men don't cry or apologize either, right? No. But that's the story we tell. It's another mix-up. Caring is women's work—perhaps the biggest and most damaging mix-up of all.

SHIFTING THE PARADIGM:
MOTHERING AS POWER, NOT DEPLETION

We often speak of mothering as a sacrifice—a one-way flow of gifts from mother to baby. We see mothers as suffering and depleted, as carrying a "mother wound" that they pass on to their daughters, generation after generation. It is true that mothers have suffered and have sacrificed. Our babies are physically and cognitively dependent on us. They require that we give them physical care, care that is not returned—until maybe in our old age if we are lucky. Early parenting requires that we feed and clean our babies, even though our babies can't and don't do that for us. That physical care is one way. With no one to care for us while we are caring for another, we are certainly left depleted, often dangerously so. But physical care alone is not mothering. Mothering is so much more.

Mothering, attunement, and the dance of affective empathy are a two-way street. They are co-creative activities. The mother receives from the baby as much as the baby receives from the mother. The most recent evolutionary and neuroscientific data suggest that there is merit to this idea—the idea that the dance of affective empathy is the opposite of depletion. In Chapter 9, we review how time spent in contact with our babies increases our oxytocin hormone levels. It's easy to see how millennia of caring have given women a biological capacity for empathy.

Unfortunately, we continue to think of mothering as one-way caring—sacrifice and depletion. In our attempt to address the injustices women have faced, especially our criminal abandonment of women who need care while they are mothering, we have thrown out the baby with the bathwater. Instead of fortifying the home, we have downgraded, passed off, and in some cases tried to eliminate the work of home. All of it, including the work of affective empathy.

With affective empathy, everyone has everything they need. Mother and child. It is perfect. It always is, was, and will be. Because connection with another human being is the nature of being human. It grows us as much as it grows them. The survival of our babies is proof. It is the armor we need as we try to make it in the world with our humanity intact. This relational currency is the seat of human power. And men deserve some too. Especially if they want to be #Sexy.

*

CHAPTER 20

The #Sexy Leader:
The Real Leader
of the Future

"How come other world leaders are so much…better, handsomer,
smarter…well, everything, than our leaders here?"
—A 14-year-old American girl

Politics these days are illuminating. Whether you hate arrogant and righteous liberals (and the "fake news" that perpetuates their mythology) or cannot stand the grating voices of right-wing heroes (and the talk show hosts who parrot them), there is a lot of "otherness" to absorb in 2018.

"My way or the highway" has penetrated into the everyday lives of voters in the US, sometimes straining friendships and making the Thanksgiving table tense among family. Whether you love or hate your job or have an evolved or ice age boss at work, we are mirroring our leaders in a way that touches us all now. So, as much as we hate politics, it is a big blessing to be talking altogether, finally, about what makes a leader a leader. Political leadership is showing us important things, and we're in a telling moment.

The US is more politically divided than it's been in a long time. The 32% approval rating for our president at the end of his first year makes him the least popular first-year president on record.[145] This news comes on the heels of record-breaking lows for both presidential candidates in the 2016 election.[146] Maybe we're jaded. Or maybe we're witnessing the last gasp of an old-style leadership. A Hail Mary play. It's not just in the United States. Nationalism and separatist movements are stirring the pot globally. Whether or not it works remains to be seen.

The traditional leader may have loved his pointy pyramid—and his alpha maleness, workaholism, monologues, hanging out on that hook alone—but the leader of the future? He's sexy. And it's time to bring on the #Sexy Leader! #Sexy Leaders draw us in more than they divide us. They empathize with us. They engage us. They co-create with us. Sometimes they even make us swoon.

To swoon is "to become enraptured."[147] We want to become enraptured by our leaders. We want them to bring us some joy. To give us a glimpse of something very different…maybe better. Something engaging. Inclusive. Something truly safe, emotionally. We can let ourselves go. Become enrapt. When a seemingly devoted father and husband, active environmentalist, and avid yoga practitioner shows up as a "leader" in the free world, he has our attention. You bet we swoon.

It's not really about sex in a physical sense. It's about so much more. Our fixation on the physical act is another mix-up. Thank you, Freud, but we're moving on. #Sexy Leadership is really about co-creation. It's about the kind of leadership that really does include everyone. The kind of leadership that starts from an emotionally full and healthy place, so that inside out, empathy flows, unencumbered, from a clean conscience. It's not that these leaders are perfect. No human being is. It's that they have, to the best of their ability, expanded their definition of humanity as they've grown. In love, not fear. So that when you and I see them, it's clear that we are included. We are invited to help co-create the future.

We are invited to engage. Not in sexual acts, but in that primal driving force of empathic co-creation. Which they model. Whether you agree with their policies and politics, the modeling of this kind of #Sexy Leadership matters. And we notice. And they notice, too.

Younger men and women are already starting to feel like different kinds of leaders. More sexy. They don't get all the credit. Changing times have served them well, as have evolving parenting practices. The old guard has some fresh moments, too, because we are all human, evolving together. We all have the superpower of empathy when we are able to access it.

While going off script at a press conference in the fall of 2017, President Donald Trump opened up about his brother who died from alcoholism at age 43.

> I had a brother, Fred. Great guy, best-looking guy, best personality— much better than mine…. But he had a problem. He had a problem with alcohol. And he would tell me: "Don't drink. Don't drink." He really helped me. I had somebody that guided me. And he had a very, very, very tough life because of alcohol. Believe me—very, very tough, tough life. He was a strong guy, but it was a tough, tough thing that he was going through. But I learned because of Fred.[148]

They say the light enters at the wound. The wound can be emotional, like losing a beloved brother. Trump reached into that pain and shared it with us for a moment. It was a difficult thing to do. But he did it. He told us how awful it was to lose Fred to addiction. And he showed us how to make meaning out of that pain, by being honest. He wasn't acting. He was there with us. It meant a lot. The answers to the opioid crisis are not simple, but honest conversation is a good start. It was a #Sexy Leader moment.

Not everyone agreed with his politics, but President Barack Obama was unassailable as a husband and father. And he let it show.

He didn't hide those qualities. Maybe we would have thought Hillary Clinton more authentic if she'd admitted to baking the occasional cookie for Chelsea. We don't know. But 59% of us approved in President Obama's final job rating (which, by the way, is relatively high…yeah, we're hard on presidents here).[149]

But let's not put too much faith in adults. The kids know what's what. Their language is affective empathy, less encumbered by the cognitive dissonance of living.

PICTURES ARE WORTH A THOUSAND WORDS.

Remember the image of the young Black boy touching President Obama's head in the Oval Office because, *finally*, a president had hair just like his? It's a cold, cold soul who wasn't moved upon seeing this image. By now you know cold soul means absence of empathy.

Those of you on the right may be paying special attention to former President George W. Bush. What's he up to these days? He is playing with grandkids and painting wounded soldiers. The quality of his soldiers in pastels is surprising art critics.

Empathy development is going on there as well. "I know each person I painted," he said. "I was thinking about their backgrounds, their service, their injuries and their recovery."[150] He is doing more feeling than thinking these days. President Bush gave up his power tools for human connection. That's a #Sexy trade-off. Can you blame us for swooning?

And what about the babies? Babies speak affective empathy better than the rest of us, as they're so undistracted by our myths. Positional authority doesn't compute yet, so leadership is pure and unfettered. It's as simple as, "Do I want to be around this guy or gal?" Here's where it gets interesting. And remarkably consistent. Babies know what's what. Google any picture of President "Donald Trump campaigning, with babies."[151] Go ahead. We'll wait.

There are so many pictures with babies crying in President Trump's arms or even merely in his presence. Sometimes Donald is crying too. Grimacing at least. These pictures seem funny. But they're not. Not for those babies at that moment. Not even for President Trump. Holding a crying baby is no fun. It makes us feel utterly powerless, impotent to help.

How can a leader build a future when children opt out? When none of what he or she builds includes the voices of the future? When he or she has walked away from the most foundational experience of all?

#NotSexy. #NotSexyAtAll.

Leaders who do not engage and co-create—leaders without empathy, really—may wield power for a time, but *leaders cannot self-appoint.* They're made by us, and we make them by choosing to pay attention. By choosing to follow, because their truth is our truth at the deepest level—beneath the narrative of our emotional injuries—deep in the well of our souls, our conscience, our shared humanity.

But it is confusing. What's #Sexy Leadership vs sex? Harvey Weinstein messed that up big time. When we idealize alpha males, we shouldn't be surprised when we get an animalistic creature who uses physical dominance to try to mate with anyone he chooses. Before we were infatuated with a romanticized version of the term, "alpha male" was used in primatology to describe chimpanzee politics.[152] But we are not chimps. We are human beings. We are more evolved, even if we don't always act like it.

Conflating power and sex is as old as time, but that doesn't make it right. Just another bad habit. Another mix-up we can make right. Right here. Right now. So, let's take it on directly.

Let's REALLY talk about sex.

*

The Future Can Be Empathic…and #Sexy

CHAPTER 21

Sex and Second Chances

"It takes two."
—Sonny and Cher[153]

I t all starts with sex. Sex is the starting point of our physical existence. Sex is also the original empathic act. The design is awesome. Body to body, skin to skin, we are driven to co-create something bigger. What if we designed home and work to look more like sex? You've always known sex was important, didn't you?

There are so many great things about sex that it is easy to lose sight of its most profound role—to make another human being. Survival of our species was clearly part of the original plan. We are driven to propagate. We are driven to bring forth the next generation. Co-creation at its most...*ehm*, naked...feels good. Thank goodness, because without sex, where would we be? Our species couldn't continue without it. Ask the Shakers. Getting rid of sex was a deal breaker for them. Have you met any lately? Neither have we.

The creation of another human being, despite our flaws and imperfect intentions, is a co-creative miracle within our capabilities but beyond our deepest understanding. Here is what we do know.

Immaculate conception aside, for as long as there have been Homo sapiens, it has taken male sperm plus a female egg to make a human baby. Some animals are capable of parthenogenesis or "virgin births"—Komodo dragons for example[154]—but so far that's not the normal way for humans.

Flora, a Komodo dragon, was able to conceive without the help of a mate, only the second time that the phenomenon of parthenogenesis has been seen in a Komodo dragon.[155]

These days, baby making can happen in a multitude of ways,[156] but there is no getting around the need for at least two people at the outset of conception. Biologically speaking, the creation of a human being is a partnership.

And an equal partnership at that. Babies get 50% of their DNA from the egg and 50% from the sperm. It is absolutely egalitarian, down to the decimal. There is no boss. There is no lead parent. Everyone matters equally. Biologically anyway. Co-creative sex is not a matriarchy, and it's not a patriarchy. No one gets exclusive rights. Power plays and manipulation of sex for profit are man-made mix-ups. Nothing divine about that.

Yet, at the end of the day, despite the baby having half of its genetics from an egg and half from a sperm, the baby is both and neither. Try to wrap your head around that. The baby is greater than the sum of its parts. It's something new, unique. A third. It exists in the space between.

> "Your children are not your children.
> They are the sons and daughters of Life's longing for itself.
> They come through you but not from you,
> And though they are with you yet they belong not to you."[157]
> —From "Children" by Khalil Gibran

...AND SECOND CHANCES

And sex can mark another kind of pivot point—a second chance at growing empathy.

Much has been written on the importance of consistent parental presence during the early years—for our children. Remember, it gives them an "internal pot of gold ... of healthy empathy." But equally important, time at home with our babies is an opportunity for us, as parents, to grow our empathy. For those of us who may not have gotten enough empathy the first time around as children, or maybe had it educated or worked out of us, parenting is a second chance. A do-over. An opportunity to rewire that part of our brain.

Because even when babies cry, throw up, and pee all over us, our overriding drive is to love and protect them. We are built that way, from the inside out. Empathy grows within the context of our most primal relationships. It's a feeling thing, not a cognitive exercise you can acquire through training at work. And if empathy is the game you are playing, this is a step you can't afford to skip.

The conscious experience of parenting, for men as well as women, gets embedded in the physical body. We can literally grow our capacity for empathy. Boys and men (and women who forgot)...can literally grow mirror neurons! Oh, yes, we can.

SURPRISE! DADS CAN GROW EMPATHY, TOO

Remember that research showing hands-on parenting increases empathy in the brain?[158] Here's the secret: It works for men, too! That's right. In men—as well as women—hormones, infant cues, and time invested in caretaking reconfigure neural networks. The work happens through skin-to-skin contact. This is good news for people without a uterus or breasts! This is good news for men. Yep, men have skin in this game.

Scientists thought of that, too, and tested new dads for levels of these empathy-related hormones as well, finding that they increased as men cohabited with moms during pregnancy, and then while holding their newborns to their bare chests after they were born. Skin to skin. Remember pheromones? Those sexy molecules infused into perfume in the 1980s? Scientists believe pheromones carry these nonverbal messages, affecting the behavior and physiology of moms and dads and babies.[159]

But wait—there's more. In the last five years, they gave fathers a turn in the fMRI machine. A slew of research showed that the brain circuits associated with empathy are engaged when fathers are exposed to their baby's cries or image. This research is quickly putting to rest the myth that only mothers can do empathy with their children. Scientist have also observed parents—both mothers AND fathers—as they interacted with their infants and babies in real time. These studies showed that the more hands-on, interactive behavior that parents engaged in, the higher their oxytocin levels. They found correlations not just with the type of behaviors parents engaged in but also in the amount of time parents spent with their children.

Empathy is a contact sport. And men get to play too. The more contact, the more empathy.

As you would expect, it's a two-way street. Kids don't learn empathy as a subject in school; they learn relationally. Early on, they absorb it, literally, in their bodies. From physical contact with parents, especially the affective part of empathy. Wonder why? As primatologist Frans de Waal puts it: "Children read 'hearts' well before they read minds."[160]

THERE'S STILL TIME

It may be the bottom of the ninth with bases loaded and two men out, but there is still time for men to turn this game around if we let biology teach us. Sex is a template for empathy. Here's Rifkin again: "Empathy requires a porous boundary between I and thou that allows the identity of two beings to mingle in a shared mental space."[161] Sounds a lot like sex to us.

What if we followed the divine, wonderful, co-creative power of biological sex as a template for how to raise our children and live our personal and professional lives? What if leadership was like sex—an equal partnership with co-creation as the goal, based in mutuality, not power? What if the evolutionary game was not so much survival of the fittest as "we are better together than alone"? Might we somehow be better off? And what would that life look like?

✳

CHAPTER 22

The Dream:
Co-creation at Home

"She's got a smile it seems to me
Reminds me of childhood memories
Where everything was as fresh as the bright blue sky"
— Guns N' Roses, "Sweet Child O' Mine," 1987

We have a dream. The dream is not really about men or women. It's about both. It's about co-creation. It's about building a life and raising children in partnership.

Sounds simple, but it's not always easy. Why is it important to dream and then realize co-creation at home? Because most of us become parents, including nine out of ten adults in the US. The desire to co-create/procreate is strong enough to overcome the fear, the day-to-day stress, and the ~$300K price tag of raising a child to 18 years old in this country (not including college). Parents who take the leap to have a baby are not what we call "rational economic actors." But we do it anyway. There must be more to life than economics, at least in the way we currently keep score.

So we have dreams.

We know it sounds crazy, but let's pretend for a moment that we *can* design work around home rather than vice versa. What would *that* look like?

A child arrives in your arms. You begin a relationship with another human being who would literally die without you. It's a lot to carry for one person. So ideally, someone else is there with you. The other parent. Or another person in the child's life with skin in the game.

It would be great if we could bring the village back to offer support from the periphery. With help from an extended family and community that has your back, you and your partner are there with the child, in the same room, ushering life into the world together. You share the tasks. You share advice. You share the emotional highs and lows. How long does this go on? Longer than you think. At least the six weeks that most people *don't* get for maternity leave in this country. Ideally even longer, because the baby wants his parents, and parents want their baby, and the whole situation is vulnerable for a good while. A year? Yeah, that would be a good length of time. It's not as crazy as it sounds. Ask your friends in Sweden, Norway, and Finland. The Dutch are world leaders here as well.

Because the earliest days are when children experience empathy from their parents. Before they have words. And parents get to practice something with baby (and with each other) that the world has beaten out of them, especially if they were born a boy. (At least now. Maybe not so much in the future.)

In this ideal scenario, there is no "lead parent." Nothing so vulnerable as one person on the hook for a whole other human being! Nothing like one person making ALL of the decisions for a brand new life—all alone. Nope. There is a solid team—a duo—the two most invested people in the child's life.

What does "invested" mean? We can answer that by asking: Who has the most to lose if this child dies? Would it be the babysitter the couple found on Care.com? Probably not. Most likely it's the parents—or just the single parent, if baby's other parent is out of the picture. Yet even when parents are not married or living together, partnership around children remains a viable option that behooves everyone. Perhaps Gwyneth Paltrow wasn't crazy or weird when she popularized the term "conscious uncoupling" as a stand-in for divorce. She was onto something—the idea that when all else fails between two people, the child remains a part of their shared meaning. Denying this truth doesn't make it go away.

The village chips in, but nobody leads at home more than parents, bringing their whole selves, undistracted. Mom doesn't know best, so she has no inclination to hog all the snuggle time. It's time women stopped being complicit in that myth too. It's not one person caring for everyone, but co-creation. Everyone helping everyone else move and grow together. Baby is growing. Parents are changing and growing—hormonally, in their brain chemistry, their hearts, and souls—synchronized with baby.

As baby grows, he moves away from parents from time to time, but comes back to touch base. That's a fundamental part of the job, actually, and one we don't discuss enough. We need to be there for our children, even when it looks like they don't need us anymore.

By toddlerhood parents are in a rhythm of sharing the work and joy, both leaning into and out of home. It's a dance. They do it together, and time inside and outside of home nourishes the work of both. Their empathy grows, big time, which makes people at work want to sign up for the incredible professional development course these parents must have taken.

Soon little Johnny will go to preschool. A really good one like the Hanna Perkins Center for Child Development in Shaker Heights, Ohio, we hope. Because they know how to handle this big step of "separation" in which Johnny learns to keep his parents in mind while he plays with friends and learns from teachers. Oh, yeah, and remembers empathy, starting with self-care. He'll know just what to do with feelings that come up. With that kind of foundation, people will later marvel at his "internal motivation" and "entrepreneurship." Oh, the places he'll go!

And then voilà! It's time for kindergarten. You can hardly believe it, but he is ready. And your feelings of sadness are tempered by joyful expectation. You've been there all along and know that this is just right. Johnny is ready for more. He can't wait to read. There is a big world to learn about and so many friends to make. The room is filled with colors, and he glances back only briefly before skipping in. Getting on the big-kid school bus has been a goal of his for years. He's finally made it!

Importantly, in this dream world, the work and school days are equal. Johnny has lots to tell after school, and parents love being there to hear it. That little break is an unexpected bonus for hardworking parents. Problems that seemed thorny at three o'clock simmer on the back burner and look easier after dinner, bath, books, and bed for Johnny. And creativity is on high. Who knew taking a break would help parents work so much more effectively and efficiently? Oh, yeah, they've proven it with research, actually.[162]

So this is how it goes, this co-creative dance. It continues for 18 years, and beyond. Just like the Game of Life. It's not over 'til it's over. Parents play their parts, and Johnny stays in the game with them. Stuff happens. Good stuff and bad stuff. He scores a hat trick in soccer! He gets familial migraines ... and you have to figure out how to solve them without drugs. He gets his favorite teacher! The next one turns out to be a miserable human being who favors girls and says hurtful stuff in the classroom. He tells you in the middle of the night, through tears, that she can't hurt him because he doesn't respect her, but he's worried about the others. You hug him tight and tear up, too, because that's just right. You work through all of it together.

The dance evolves. The music changes key. The lead shifts away from the parents to the kids. Sometimes one parent has to carry on after another dies. Sometimes one parent is all the kid has from the get-go. The dance may be lonelier and harder—with more back-up dancers in the routine—but still nobody leaves the floor. And life goes on. Aging parents/grandparents bring unique contributions and needs. But the gift, the real gift that makes the dream possible in all of its glory no matter what happens...is time. Time for parents and children together.

> *"I hear babies crying, I watch them grow*
> *They'll learn much more than I'll never know*
> *And I think to myself what a wonderful world*
> *Yes I think to myself what a wonderful world"*
> — Louis Armstrong "What a Wonderful World," 1967

IT'S ABOUT TIME

Time is so difficult to come by these days that you'll need to explicitly focus on it. Before parents can play jazz, they will likely need to practice with sheet music together. Explicit conversations about who does what, when in the home and especially with the children. In good times and in bad. In sickness and in health. You are family now and need to renew your vows, with baby in the picture.

Hopefully, the world won't always make it so hard for parents to find time for what matters most. Hopefully *soon*, the world will even support that work, because *the time warp is coming*. The dream of co-creation at home will be possible. And guess what: Empathy is the way to get more of the time you desperately need, while you wait for the world to change

Next, we will discuss how to find or make a workplace that invests in empathy. We do not always have choices at work, but sometimes we do. At the margin, we should always be moving toward "The New Way to Work." Like at home, there should be co-creation at work, too.

CHAPTER 23

The Dream:
Co-creation at Work

The world is changing fast, but the time warp has not yet arrived. We still have to go to work. Most of our factories, offices, hospitals, etc. are not fertile ground for dream jobs. So what can we do at work right now to preserve and grow our empathy? Is there some way to design work around our humanity rather than vice versa? Can we be successful while preserving our soul? Can we succeed by coming together to co-create at work rather than competing against each other? In our experience, it is possible but not easy. Because it requires that we go against the existing culture. That can be hard. You have to be brave, but it's worth it.

If you ever liked any of your jobs at some point in your life, you probably remember that it had a lot to do with the people around you. There were probably certain relationships that stood out. You remember:

- That time you shared shifts with _____, who would have been your friend even if he wasn't your coworker. You made each other laugh. Time flew by.

- That project which turned out better than anything one of you might have designed, because all voices really were included.

You could hardly believe it.

- That year when your team in the _____ department really had each other's backs. It took a while for you to realize it, but it was true. It hasn't been the same since you got transferred, but the feeling of working that well together is something you've been trying to find ever since. Work didn't feel like work. It was fun.

But then again, we have all had times with colleagues that made us hurt. You remember:

- The colleague who worked so closely with you, he knew all of your strengths and weaknesses. It was no problem, until he got jealous of your new job and knew just how to sabotage your work.

- That time your co-worker pinned you against the wall at the holiday party, because after a few drinks, the co-creative way you had been working together got mixed up in his mind with the kind of co-creation he practiced with his wife. He even used the word love; it was confusing.

- That time your husband accused you of having an affair with a man at work who captured a lot of your attention and time because working together was so fulfilling. You didn't do anything wrong, but it's hard to imagine platonic co-creation, because we're still culturally stunted.

Getting co-creation just right at work—appropriately close, #Sexy without the sex—can be tricky. It's tricky not because we are incapable as humans, but because our cultural myths at home and systems at work trip us up. Empathy helps us break through the confusion, individually and systemically.

OPENING UP TO EMPATHY IN THE WORKPLACE

In the best situations, people at work are able to steward a different kind of currency, something *beyond* money. This "currency of empathy" counterbalances our common and pervasive mix-ups about leadership and work, time, and yes, even sex. Individuals can steward empathy; but wouldn't it be great if organizations did that, too? Wouldn't it be great if we didn't have to fight against culture to feel human? Wouldn't it be great if co-creativity at home could reinforce co-creativity at work in the office and vice versa? Work might even be fun!

Organizations CAN steward a "currency of empathy." It's simple, but it's not easy. The keys to ushering in more empathy fly in the face of decades of research and advice about how organizations should run and how leaders should lead.

Remember the pointy pyramid and what that does to leadership? (See Chapter 2 for how our leadership models and organizations sap empathy.) Leadership in the pointy pyramid is "my way or the highway." There is no time or room to consider anyone else's hopes and dreams. In the pointy pyramid, leaders treat their employees like widgets. There is no space for investing in individual development. Pointy pyramid leadership is fueled by workaholism or time spent at the office. Home only gets in the way.

But things are starting to change now. Investing in empathy means more:

1. shared meaning,
2. individual growth, and
3. ability to be whole.

Let's examine each of these benefits.

Shared Meaning

Old notions of *leadership and work* are giving way to the kind of shared meaning that truly brings people together to do things they cannot do alone. We are drawn to work in groups because of the power of humanity more than economies of scale. Organizations that steward empathy bring people together to do something bigger and better than any one person could do alone. They are in the business of making the world a better place. Money is the means, not the end. For instance, Whole Foods is transforming our food system and our health, not just profiting from grocery sales.

Often, however, "shared meaning" is just window dressing. Many ad agencies, PR firms, and investor relations folks are in that line of work, spinning products or services that really aren't so good for us. Remember that old Coca-Cola commercial with people who'd "like to teach the world to sing" by giving everyone a...brown synthetic drink with mysterious ingredients starting with high-fructose corn syrup? What? We bought that? Hey, we were young.

Meaning helps get us up in the morning. It makes us love our jobs. It makes us want to give it our all. It makes us feel good about ourselves. It aligns with our conscience. What organization wouldn't benefit from that?

Individual Growth

Organizations that steward empathy stop wasting time and *help people grow*. Revenues will follow. Remember, empathy is selfish first. So people need to be professionally fed, nurtured, and educated to acquire the tools that will allow them to succeed. Apprenticeship is a big part of it. Development conversations should be more about growth than judgment, nurturing what's special in each person, which is a shift from the habitual way. Done right, this kind of learning supports cognitive empathy, and that's a beautiful thing.

More often than not, however, organizations actively stunt professional growth. We write our own annual reviews, because how can bosses know so many of us after all that reorganizing? It's really every man for himself here. The end-of-year conversation is more about judgment than anything else. How we rank. Our bonus. Whether we'll be top-graded out this year. And on the front line, workers are valued as units of production rather than people. They feel it.

What does this do for us? It undermines our agency and destroys our inner motivation. But when our growth is an organization's priority, we feel empowered and motivated to contribute. It makes all the difference.

One interesting question to ask a prospective employer is this: Would you please tell me about your family? If they don't have much to say, run the other way. Someone who allocates no time to growing people at home won't invest much in you, either.

Ability to Be Whole

The best organizations *value whole people, include them fully, and co-create amazing futures together.* They take a clue from the most divinely creative thing we do, without even knowing how. They value you, not just professionally but also personally. They allow you to be authentic because they know there is power in that. No need to unzip that work armor and decompress with a beer when you get home. It's not even a matter of oft-cited "balance," because home and work are not a trade-off but a mutually beneficial dance. Such organizations understand that your home, where your most important relationships live, provides the juice of affective empathy that is a crucial ingredient to economic success.

How do great companies do this? They don't do it by giving you a great cafeteria and bocce court so that you end up loving work so much that you never want to go home again. No. Great companies support affective empathy by giving you the time you need at home to ensure that everyone there, including you, can lean into important relationships. And they allow you to bring that experience to work. In fact, they welcome and embrace your life experience as vital to your development and see it as valuable data for the wise decisions you will make.

Yes, these are the companies that allow—that *welcome*—your conscience in the room. No need to keep that funny lady, gay man, or proud Black father under wraps. Or the fact that we may be fathers or mothers struggling with sick kids, snow days, leaky breasts, or the increasing needs of parents with declining health. All of that becomes fair game.

When companies value whole people, they don't end up with depleted automatons. They get real people who bring all of their gifts to work. Especially their souls. Any company would be lucky to have a few more people like that.

A workplace that encourages a currency of empathy overall supports intrinsic motivation. Intrinsic motivation occurs when an individual performs according to a set of internal and authentic principles that were created over a lifetime of experience. A currency of empathy puts its faith in the idea that people have what it takes to make a valuable contribution, as long as they are supported. No need to provide the carrots and sticks. It trusts that people are reliable because they have developed their own rewards and punishments inside. It views the conscience as a critical piece of data and encourages people to access this conscience in their decision-making processes. External carrots and sticks are used to override our internal resources as a way of controlling us, as a way of rendering us powerless. Carrots and sticks dehumanize people and allow others to utilize them. And when the carrot/stick operating structure is withdrawn, the entire system collapses. Of course, sustainability is not possible.

So it's simple really, but it's not easy because the underlying solutions fly in the face of decades of advice and research about management. If your workplace comes up short, please don't despair. You are in excellent and widespread company if work doesn't give you all of that juice. Most of us work, have worked, or will work for organizations that get a lot of these three things wrong. Sometimes just a little sideways. Sometimes egregiously so.

Most organizations get some of these things somewhat right and some kinda not. But if you are one of the lucky ones whose work supports these three pillars of the Currency of Empathy® (meaning, growth, being whole), *we bet you love your job.* We're happy for you. We also bet your organization is innovative, because remember, empathy is the missing link to sustained innovation. And that innovation is what fuels the long-term financial sustainability everyone wants but has trouble achieving. Empathy is the missing link to that ever-elusive diversity and inclusion, too. If you get all of this at work, we bet you'll never leave. People stay or go based on how companies do on these three things. Take note, diversity czars and boardrooms of white men scratching your heads about why you can't keep and promote women and people of color. *Psst—you're losing the best white men too, emotionally, if not physically.* Because talented people with options leave. And talented people who don't have options create them.

We call them entrepreneurs.

*

CHAPTER 24

Entrepreneurs with Soul

An entrepreneur is "someone with the soul of an
artist whose means of expression happens to be business."
—Bernie Goldhirsh, *founding editor of* Inc. *magazine*

We love entrepreneurs. We exalt them. The US, especially, is built on them. We hold successful entrepreneurs in high regard: Henry Ford, Steve Jobs, Mark Zuckerberg, Warren Buffet, Oprah. But what is it, really, that draws us to the entrepreneur like bees to honey? What makes us want to be near them and be like them?

Is it the money? It sure is shiny—but it's kind of a tease. It's not shared. So much "entrepreneurship" is about chasing the capital and profiting by exploiting other people for their costly addictions (what we call revenues) with cheap labor (costs). Revenues minus costs = profits. That's the math we use to justify and celebrate the new egg-freezing technology (so we can work without those pesky personal relationships getting in the way), or spaceships for private tours to Mars (for those who are rich enough to make it out before our planet is officially uninhabitable).

We exalt patentable technology, but at the core, the entrepreneurship we love the most is a kind of art. And art is "channel[ing] cosmos into the chaos," according to Madeleine L'Engle.[163] These entrepreneurs do well. And they do good. The ones who capture our heads and our hearts are not just the ones who do something new, something never seen before. They are also doing something to make the world a better place. And they are doing it with soul.

These people seem to do the impossible. They make money, but that's not the point. They are motivated by *meaning*; the money is just a way of funding that work. Meaning that aligns with our empathic insides—our conscience. We envy the chance to *live like that*, not just in our spare time, but in our work, which makes up the bulk of our waking hours.

There are encouraging examples all around us. You believe the Dalai Lama that meditation can change your life, but don't know how? There's an app for that, thanks to Headspace. Don't know whom or what to trust anymore in the news? Check into Medium.com; it's a conversation and you're invited. Want to nourish your body and soul? Whether you shop at Whole Foods or not, you can be thankful for the influence they've had on our food-supply chain. We have more choices than ever for organic, non-GMO, plant-based products that make our guts happy rather than leaky and treat our bodies with respect. Sorry, Monsanto, Pepsi, and McDonald's. We're woke. So you see, money is the least enduring thing a successful entrepreneur leaves behind. They *change us*.

> "What you leave behind is not what is engraved in stone
> monuments, but what is woven into the lives of others."
> —Pericles

What else do entrepreneurs with soul do?

They work, not as bosses, but as partners. They treat their employees as people they can listen to and learn from personally and for the company's sake. Or even better, they have equal partners, not just employees. At least one "co-," a co-president, co-CEO, co-author…a co-creator. Someone they can trust. Someone who will tell them the truth. Someone who can help them *grow*, not just in size, but in ways that will equip them to continue their work with soul.

Because doing something really new and groundbreaking is tough. Nothing is certain, and the pace of change is great. The risk of failure lurks in every corner. Setbacks are the rule, not the exception. Without a true partner in your corner helping you out, who knows what you might resort to? In the face of fear and emotional scarcity, we are known to do some desperate things. Maybe you will quit because it is too hard. Maybe the fear will cause you to take shortcuts, compromising your original, more noble intentions. You might start trusting the wrong people. Hey, who's that coming up from behind?! You're scared, so you run faster or rather grow, grow, grow, in size that is. ASAP! You start to resort to external capital, which is great if it comes with real partners. But often, it doesn't. It's just hungry for more capital. Not all boards of advisors will be wed to your meaning, model, or customers. They want returns, yesterday! So now you are not just compromising. You are bastardizing. Not to mention that the pace is all consuming. You are on the hook, all the time, by yourself. Forget sleep and your personal life.

With partnership, we see something different. A culture that puts relationships first will attract others. More people get involved. The work grows. But these entrepreneurs don't grow for the sake of growth alone. Or glory. Or empire building. Or even shareholder value. They grow with intent. Because the product or service is great and more people need it. Because people want to be part of that team. They don't take outside capital if it pivots them from their passion and mission. They grow into *Small Giants.* You can read about some great examples (Patagonia, Cliff Bars, Zingerman's Deli, etc.) in the 10th anniversary edition of Bo Burlingham's book of the same name.

The best thing about entrepreneurship is you get to operate outside of the system and are not bound by the antiquated frameworks that stifle so many organizations these days. Yes, entrepreneurship can be a beautiful thing, especially when it comes to work-life balance. And more people are taking this entrepreneurship option, especially women, across the globe.

Entrepreneurship is the modern way to resolve today's disconnect between work and family. Being able to work meaningfully yet flexibly is gold for working parents. The flexibility afforded by entrepreneurship can create a workplace that values whole people and promotes diversity. Did you know that female-led businesses have grown five times the national average since the 2008–09 recession? According to the 2017 State of Women-Owned Businesses Report, the number of women-owned firms increased by 114% between 2007 and 2017. We number 11.6 million firms and generate more than $1.7 trillion in revenues.[164] Even more impressive, female minority-owned businesses have increased by 467% during the same period. Venture capital gets a disproportionate amount of attention, but entrepreneurship doesn't always require a capital investment. That's good, because minorities and women, typically disadvantaged in the capital markets, can still play. It's often easier to succeed when your client, patient, or supplier decides your fate rather than the middle manager schooled in a big-business system.

The next generation gets it. According to MiLLENNiAL magazine, "60% of Millennials consider themselves entrepreneurs, and 90% recognize entrepreneurship as a mentality."[165] Mom and dad may scratch their heads when tweens aspire to be YouTubers instead of doctors and lawyers.

Bosses bristle when young people leave for yoga or dinner with friends at 5:00 p.m. But, even while they frustrate and confuse us, the Millennials are showing us a new way (more on that in the last chapter). It's not laziness so much as entrepreneurship.

We get distracted by the shiny coins and the hype, but if you look beyond the money and technology, people all around us are successful entrepreneurs. They are:

- The immigrants who walked away from the assembly line with nothing but chutzpah and the vow, "I don't work for nobody," then built successful _____ (restaurants, grocery stores, real estate businesses, dry cleaners, nail salons, etc.) and helped their cousins immigrate and thrive in similar businesses

- The adult daughter of an alcoholic who builds a thriving therapy practice helping families move beyond the pain she knows all too well

- The yoga teacher who leaves the Hamptons (New York) for the Hampton Inn (Beachwood, Ohio) to help people in her hometown discover the lifeblood that transformed her

- The consultant who leaves the security of a big firm for more flexible and meaningful work when the baby arrives…even though making ends meet is not guaranteed

- The parents who become co-CEOs/partners of a _____ (magazine, sustainability consulting firm, nonprofit, science center, farm, etc.) because there is a need bigger than any one person can fill, while continuing to care for children and to grow their superpower of affective empathy

But entrepreneurship isn't enough. What happens when the entrepreneurial company grows and morphs into something else—namely, a large organization? What happens if you are unable to be an entrepreneur and must instead work for one of those large companies, which control so much money, people, and power? If we are to turn the global *Titanic* around before we hit the iceberg, large organizations must be transformed as well.

So let's take a look inside bigger companies.

CHAPTER 25

Intrapreneurs with Mojo

"That used to be us..."

—CEO *of $35-million family-owned electronics business*

It doesn't take long for small, nimble, entrepreneurial ventures to turn corporate. Because you know what they say: "Growth is good! Growth is necessary! Economies of scale lower costs and make business models profitable." Unfortunately, the things that make us fall in love with entrepreneurs are often the things that get contorted when the business grows. Often, it is the soul that gets lost on the way to the big leagues.

PART I: ENTREPRENEURS GROW UP TO BE INTRAPRENEURS...OR MANAGERS

Many of us continue to admire entrepreneurs who evolve their business into a large organization. We admire them because they get rich. Very rich. Entrepreneurship is a game, and some people win big. Like in Monopoly. And if you started playing, investing, accruing interest, and accumulating real estate, houses, and hotels on Boardwalk and Park Place 200 years before the rest of us, you are probably even richer now. Perhaps we shouldn't be so impressed.

We also admire them for the jobs they create. While job creation is good, when entrepreneurs extract more value than they share, that's not so good. How can we know if this is the case? It's hard to numerically assess whether labor wages accurately reflect the value of the work being performed. But when we look at the difference between CEO pay and worker pay, something doesn't sit right. According to recent data, CEOs earn 331 times as much as average workers, and 774 times as much as minimum-wage earners.[166] That's just not okay. And we have to wonder: How do CEOs in opulent houses keep their consciences clear when their employees—the very people who made their entrepreneurial dreams come true—can't keep the lights on at home or send their kids to a decent school?

You see, the numerically positive math of profits = revenues minus costs doesn't always tell the whole story. It doesn't account for our conscience. It is not clear that we should celebrate the billionaire opening a new casino focused on "increasing the wallet share of heavy users" (addicts, we call them) without including a nagging conscience to the debit side of our ledger.

But alas, there is a solution to the conscience problem. It's called philanthropy. It's hard not to admire entrepreneurs for that. Cancer hospitals, vaccines for children in Tanzania. If arts and crafts are your thing, it's the vibrant summer festival in your sleepy little town that you applaud. What could possibly be wrong with THAT? Well, nothing. People giving money to the causes most near and dear to their hearts is just right. It is when we have skin in the game that philanthropy is most powerful and effective.

The problem is that your near-and-dear is not always my near-and-dear. I don't always have skin in your game. And when the 100 wealthiest people in the US own more wealth than the entire Black population, that becomes a problem.[167] Philanthropy morphs into something ugly—into tech billionaires siphoning huge resources toward the science of living forever when Black babies in Cleveland, Ohio, are dying at alarming rates. It morphs into the unconscionable act of a wealthy few setting the educational, health, science, etc. agenda for the rest of us, when they don't even know us. So you see, philanthropy is more complicated than we would like to believe. It really doesn't absolve us of anything. Maybe our conscience would have been better off if we had shared the wealth upstream—when the company janitor really needed the money.

SIZE DOES MATTER—BIGGER IS NOT ALWAYS BETTER

According to Yuval Harari in *Sapiens*:

> *Sociological research has shown that the maximum "natural" size of a group ... is 150 individuals. Most people can neither intimately know, nor gossip effectively about, more than 150 human beings. Even today, a critical threshold in human organizations falls somewhere around this magic number. Below this threshold, communities, businesses, social networks, and military units can maintain themselves based mainly on intimate acquaintance and rumour-mongering. There is no need for formal ranks, titles, and law books to keep order. ...A small family business can survive and flourish without a board of directors, a CEO, or an accounting department. But once the threshold of 150 individuals is crossed, things can no longer work that way. Successful family businesses usually face a crisis when they grow larger and hire more personnel. If they cannot reinvent themselves, they go bust.[168]*

So, what do we do when our company grows? We make quick work of *professionalizing* our company as it scales. We come up with rules that order our work lives to manage this new scale. Business schools teach them. Consultants spread them like viruses from company to company. We tell ourselves that cash is king, top-grading is leadership development, and workaholism is something to be exploited. Business schools pit people against their peers, which becomes vital practice for the years to come as designated "leaders" rise through the ranks. Productivity, command and control, and leaning in are all the rage. We drive efficiency, and we do it well. Not just in business, but in schools, in nonprofits, and in churches. Oh, and schools and daycare, too, where kids become "units."

You name it, we've professionalized it. This isn't all bad, but a lot of it is not good, either. Business as usual is empathy sapping. Businesses have been focused on making money, not growing empathy. We're reaping precisely what we've sown. It worked for a while, for some people anyway. Sometimes we think that once we get to the top, we'll change things. But what usually happens is that the system changes *us* first. And we manage. Just the way we've been taught to do.

It's just not working anymore. Walking into most large organizations makes us hurt. That's why we check out mentally or physically. That's why we lack the trust needed to drive real innovation. And it's hitting the bottom line. The lifetime of a corporation on the S&P 500 is steadily declining. If you work in a large organization, perhaps you stay up at night, wondering if your company will be the next one to fail. If you are on the leadership team, maybe you worry it will be on your watch.

So, you have three choices. You can:

1. abide and manage;
2. leave; or
3. become an intrapreneur—someone who creates change from the inside out, at scale. An entrepreneur on the inside.

Intrapreneurship is not for the faint-hearted. People hate change, so the work of an intrapreneur feels a lot like Sisyphus pushing that rock up the hill...for eternity.[169] Argh.

It's hard. It's sometimes dangerous. You might get crushed. And it's been confusing in the last few years, too. Lots of people have hopped on the intrapreneurship bandwagon. "Innovation inside! Disrupt yourself! Change is good!"

But to what end? So you can develop "innovative new products" that help your revenues grow?

Seriously? Do Jacked Doritos count as innovation? The ingredients include monosodium glutamate and Red #40, among other toxins. Is that intrapreneurship (entrepreneurship inside a large organization) with soul?

Well, if it improves shareholder value and increases the CEO bonus it must be good, right?

Ah, no.

Luckily for Frito-Lay, the biggest downstream costs of Jacked Doritos (and all of their other products) are tucked beyond their own P&L, in our supersized health-care budget.

PART II: INTRAPRENEURS WITH SOUL

But there are intrapreneurs inside fighting the good fight. Intrapreneurs with mojo—with *soul*—who make changes that lead to longer-term sustainability for companies, and increased empathy. They achieve longer-term sustainability *because* they increase empathy. These are intrapreneurs leading innovation with soul. That's the key here. With soul. With a conscience. Because what good is a disrupter without soul? It's a disruption. A distraction. A diversion. A sideshow. Innovation with soul is art inside of corporations. It's rare. It's:

- The woman who works to streamline the FDA so lifesaving technologies can be available to more people, faster

- The man who leverages his corporate platform to improve the community in ways no one has tried, gathering fellows of every stripe as he goes

- The public school administrator who somehow manages to intimately know each and every student, out of hundreds, even making sure the vulnerable ones are fed on a daily basis

- The distinguished engineering professor whose brilliance is a given, but whose humanity really sets him apart and guides all of his work

- The public radio executive who, once and for all—really, truly—wants to build an enterprise that includes *everyone* in the community

Maybe you're that guy or gal. If so, thank you.

It's not easy fighting the good fight. It's an uphill battle to move the powers- and assets-that-be in new directions. Here are some things we've noticed about you, intrapreneur with soul:

- You have vision, insight, and foresight. We think you're channeling something. How else do you see it before everyone else?

- You are patient because organizations usually make progress more slowly than you'd like.

- You're persuasive. Often, you don't have positional authority, but you get the job done anyway.

- You're centered and optimistic. You have to be, because you are not always appreciated and are sometimes feared, or worse, marginalized.

- You have faith and courage—not the blind kind, but the kind that sees clearly, acknowledges fear, and moves forward anyway.

- You do not work alone. That wouldn't be any fun. Plus, what you try to do is bigger than any one person.

But what is most marvelous about you is how you've retained your humanity. Your conscience is intact. How did you do it? You made trade-offs. They weren't easy. You turned down that promotion so that you wouldn't have to move the kids in the middle of high school. You skirted or even left the corner office and found the nanny a new job when your kids needed you. You pushed the boundaries to help in ways that only you can, like taking your aging mom to her heart doctor.

The true leaders aren't always who we think they are. We're not fooled by titles, and neither are you. The air is thin at the top of the ladder. We can't expect the most exciting and earnest change to come from there most of the time. We're watching YOU, intrapreneur.

You work with soul. You steward humanity, even in a big company where it's no longer automatic for people to know each other. You do it in big (e.g., leading company-wide initiatives) and small (e.g., how you treat people every day) ways. It's simple really, but it's not easy because the underlying solutions fly in the face of decades of advice and research about how leaders should lead and how organizations should work. But you don't care about that stuff. Those theories come and go. You pay more attention to what feels right. Your conscience. Your empathy.

Keep on keeping on, Intrapreneur with Soul. Know that you're not crazy. The world is moving your way. Your way of working will improve the bottom line and drive our economy to the next level. You'll be proven right in the end. But please, don't go it alone. Surround yourself with people who will help you be brave. And partner with them. Really. Not just pretend. You'll solve a lot more than just logistical issues when you do. Absolute power does corrupt—it corrupts our humanity by sapping our capacity for empathy.

Why did we ever think a pyramid was a good organizational shape? Why would we expect creativity from the "guy on the hook"?

No, "co" is the only way to go. When you get to be co-CEO, get loud. The world needs to hear your story.

Intrapreneurs make innovation possible. Not the fake kind of "innovation," baked into the numbers to fool the analysts, even though it's really just more cost-cutting or merger math dressed up like real growth. You lead the real kind of innovation, which results in sustainable evolution of a company through truly new products, services, and ways of doing business.

You are the kind of co-creative leader we need now and going forward. People see it, even if they can't quite put it into words yet. You've got mojo. You. Are. #Sexy. In the right way, the co-creative way. You practice partnership all the time, so you never forget that co-creation is the game.

We've long known what we really admire in leaders. Men and women. Real leaders include all of us—the children, especially. We just thought that was impossible in the old way to work. A catch-22. But it's not, not anymore.

The age of the #Sexy Leader is here. Let's find them. Let's grow them. Let's elect them. Or: Be one.

> *He achieved success who has lived*
> *well, laughed often, and loved much;*
>
> *Who has enjoyed the trust of pure women,*
> *the respect of intelligent men and*
> *the love of little children;*
>
> *Who has filled his niche and*
> *accomplished his task;*
>
> *Who has never lacked appreciation of*
> *Earth's beauty or failed to express it;*
>
> *Who has left the world better than he found it,*
>
> *Whether an improved poppy, a*
> *perfect poem, or a rescued soul;*
>
> *Who has always looked for the best in*
> *others and given them the best he had;*
>
> *Whose life was an inspiration;*
>
> *Whose memory a benediction.*
>
> *—Bessie Anderson Stanley, "Success," 1904*

Positional authority and real leadership have nothing in common, really. In fact, they are often inversely correlated. So yes, you, too, can be a #Sexy Leader by channeling some cosmos into the chaos of your own corner of the world, at work and at home. In person and online. Whether you cashier, wait tables, blog, or have a corner office. You can grow your empathy. You can help others grow theirs. You can be part of evolving humanity toward ever better and more universal truth.

It's important work.

And the kids are watching.

CHAPTER 26

An Optimistic View of the Future, i.e., Millennials Are Not Lazy

Here is the best news of all. This is much bigger than us. Over the long arc of human history, we have been moving toward greater understanding of ourselves and others. We have been moving from scarcity to abundance as a whole, although not everyone feels it yet. As Jeremy Rifkin shows in *Empathic Civilization*, we humans have been moving toward an ever-greater empathic consciousness. It's hard to imagine in the midst of current events, but history is so much bigger than this moment.

From the physical development of our brains, to the new ways we have found to communicate with each other, we've been growing our capacity for empathy and innovation. From the radical idea that marriage can be a partnership rooted in love, to the very recent notion of childhood being different from other times in a human life, we've been growing our capacity for empathy. And our global potential for empathy is increasingly buoyed by our current interconnectedness. Regardless of whether you want to retrench or favor globalization, the genie is out of the bottle. We are connected in ways we cannot unwind. We are moving irreversibly toward global consciousness, toward an Age of Empathy.

But here's the bad news: It's not inevitable that we'll get there in time to avoid another Dark Age. If fact, so many news headlines today are signposts heading in the wrong direction.

Still. Now—after so much...uhm, progress.

> *"Is it silly, no?*
> *When a rocket blows and everybody still wants to fly*
> *Some say man ain't happy truly until a man truly dies*
> *Oh why, oh why? Sign o' the times, unh"*
> —Prince, "Sign o' the Times," 1987

HOW DID WE GET HERE?

A generally rising capacity for empathy does not preclude spectacular violence, which is on view 24/7 in our interconnected world. Our far-reaching network is capable of fueling and spreading violent behavior as well as good. And the violence is both more distributed and dangerous. It's atomized and democratic. It's more entrepreneurial than state-led. The threat of terrorism feels real and present in the lives of our children—who regularly practice "active shooter drills" in school—as does the possibility of nuclear annihilation. And terrorism can be inspired and even enabled online, millions of miles away. It's hard to be comforted by statistics that were based on organized warfare and historic crime categories when our brave new world has different rules and is, ironically, innovative in violence. Those stats are obsolete.

Neuroscience professor Simon Baron-Cohen has shown a correlation between evil behavior and absence of empathy, which he calls zero empathy.[170] In science, there is no such thing as cold, only absence of heat. No such thing as dark, only absence of light. Similarly, perhaps evil can be explained as a void—of empathy. It makes a lot of sense. And we see the portrait of a psychopath as a young man (hardly any women perpetuate violence ... see Chapter 15) emerging time and again, with empathy deficit disorder rising throughout his life experience (e.g., consider the long line of "loners," from Dylan Klebold who shot up the Columbine school to Micah Xavier Johnson, who ambushed Dallas police, killing five, in July 2016). Interestingly, racial and demographic lines blur. Psychologically, they have a lot in common.

And as such, while we worry about the evil—zero empathy—acts of violence out there, we should worry even more about *situational and cultural* empathy deficits that affect all of us and push some people over the edge. We should be concerned with the systems that act on people, who may start out with good intentions but have little time to invest in their humanity and empathy. The network moves with all of us, and we dial in the culture and kin we have online. Empathy deficits can grow (they look and feel more like fear and anger) as easily as empathy surpluses (which look and feel more like hope and love).

The future is up to us. Even more, it's up to our millennial daughters, sons, granddaughters, neighbors, and friends. So, it's important to ask:

Is empathy rising with every subsequent generation, or not?

Here's where things can get confusing, but we must try to sort it out. The answer to this question is key to the future. It's easy to find psychological studies in which Millennials are maligned as the most narcissistic generation ever. Why, here's one now: Professor Sara Konrath and her associates at the Institute for Social Research at the University of Michigan recently surveyed 13,000 college students, and found them to be "40% lower in empathy than their counterparts of 20 or 30 years ago." She concluded that "young adults today comprise one of the most self-concerned, competitive, confident, and individualistic cohorts in recent history."[171]

OUCH.

But wait a minute: 13,000 people cannot adequately represent 80 million, right? And we're not so worried about university students who are focused on themselves and their studies. That's kind of their job, isn't it? Growing SELF. And remember, empathy is selfish first. Without a well-developed sense of self, mature empathy is not possible. You can't really put yourself in anyone else's shoes unless your own foundation is solid.

A more recent and nuanced look at Millennials is the Pew Research Center's sequence of reports on Millennials. The 2010 edition, subtitled "Confident. Connected. Open to Change," offers a very different view of a diverse, introspective, complex generation. One that weathered September 11th and has been wired since childhood. They are skeptical of institutions, including political and religious. They are focused on acquiring less, not more: "Almost two-thirds (64 percent) of millennials said they would rather make $40,000 a year at a job they love than $100,000 a year at a job they think is boring."[172]

Any anthropologist will tell you that we can learn a lot about people by looking at the food they eat. Here is where Millennials really shine. They take health and environmental stewardship to a new level. "For millennials, food isn't just food. It's community," we hear from the Pew report. And are they absorbing the nutritional and environmental truths finally unfolding after 50 years of "better living through chemistry" (like the DuPont slogan says) and decades of Big Ag with pesticides, hormones, depleted soil, and GMOs (thanks to Monsanto and others)? No! An estimated 12% of Millennials are "faithful vegetarians and even vegan," compared with 4% of Gen Xers and 1% of Baby Boomers, according to one study.

All in all, we agree with the *New York Times* observation, "Taken together, these habits and tastes look less like narcissism than communalism. And its highest value isn't self-promotion, but its opposite, empathy—an open-minded and -hearted connection to others."[173]

Ah. Yeah. There. Millennials get the credit they deserve for empathy. We've noticed some other things as well that suggest a wholesale rejection of the competitive status quo. Maybe the fact that they hold out for meaningful work is a sign of evolution toward greater empathic consciousness. Maybe their parents were evolved, too, compared to our parents' generation, for whom spanking was still normal. In any case, we do not believe the rap that Millennials are lazy. We think empathy may become your "secret sauce."

Author and executive coach Ray Williams, in *Psychology Today*, sums it up nicely:

Are we becoming more narcissistic, less empathetic, led by GenMe, or are we moving toward a more empathetic age, one that has social justice, social responsibility, sustainability and concern for our environment as of paramount importance? It seems to me that both things are happening. We are moving to a new age of social concerns, while at the same time, the last throes of narcissistic, materialistic and "externally focused" values are embraced. A contradiction? Paradox? Perhaps, but thus is the nature of our universe.[174]

Do the results of the 2016 US Presidential election say anything? Millennials voting overwhelmingly Democratic. Millennials protesting and speaking out against the eruption of -isms. Perhaps the results indicate their lack of "experience" in the world. "How quaint! That used to be us," we may think. "They'll grow out of it." We're sure because most of us did.

But maybe they won't. And maybe that's exactly what the world needs. Not another generation jaded by experience and sapped of empathy, but something very different. Something better and more evolved. Perhaps coming of age in the crucible of a world that so clearly and loudly grates on their conscience will forge them into diamonds.

Maybe growing in collective reaction to something—even big mix-ups—is a kind of gift. It can be clarifying.

THE FUTURE IS IN THEIR HANDS

In any case, the way the world goes will depend very much on what the next generation of "leaders"—the Millennials—DO. And we are *not* talking about profession. Their empathic secret sauce is not fully cooked. So the next question to ask is how *can* Millennials grow their empathy? (Hint: Posting daily pics of their kids on Facebook won't do it.)

They'll probably end up sitting in on one of those increasingly popular and lucrative empathy-training classes at some point. We hope their affective empathy is in good shape by then, so the cognitive tools might help more than hurt. Like knife-skills training before you grab the Wüsthof chef's knife and start chopping. Remember that mature, full-bodied empathy (affective and cognitive) is something that is developed over time through real-life experience in relationship to others.

Empathy Is a Contact Sport

You can't so much train empathy INTO people as make room for them to practice it. It bears repeating again and again: No amount of empathy training at work can match *caring* for people in real life!

We hope by now you see clearly that the most formative and profound of these empathy-building experiences happens at home between parents and children. As a whole, it is likely that Millennials got more than prior generations did. Parenting practices have evolved over the last few decades to become more empathic and less patriarchal. Spanking is only recently out of vogue.

But no parents are perfect, so thankfully there are still many opportunities for you to grow empathy muscles even today, no matter what your generation. First, remember that empathy begins within, so take care of yourself. Eat well, exercise, get your sleep, do yoga, meditate, read good books, be with nature...and surround yourself with good friends. Make time for them and take care of each other. And as time goes on, the people in your life may expand to include spouses, long-term partners, and children. It is likely that the stakes in your relationships will grow, and with those greater stakes come greater challenges but also more opportunity for personal growth. Parenting is a big one. When we become parents to children, we are offered perhaps the second biggest opportunity to develop our empathy after childhood. The research will keep rolling in to support this fact...grandmothers will keep scratching their heads at the need for it.

So, what should you do if you are a young person today? Choose education and work that gives you meaning, helps you grow, and lets you be a whole person. Work hard, learn a ton, and become as excellent as you can while taking good care of yourself. Doing excellent work early on earns you flexibility and freedom later. But don't do that thing that so many GenXers did. Where you work 100 hours a week at a job that pays well but destroys your health and well-being—not to mention does a number on your conscience. Don't leave it to your kids to teach YOU about eating and sleeping properly when they come along. That's a big burden. And it gets in the way of your empathy and the success you were shooting for in the first place.

We realize that parenting as a path to empathic development does not mean much to a young, single person today, but we hope you'll tuck that fact away, because in 5 or 10 or 15 years, you will need it. And so will your kids. Your neighbors. Your bosses. Maybe your grandkids.

And surround yourself with good role models. If you have the good fortune to someday welcome young children into this world, find yourselves some men and women who act like menopausal whales. That's right. Whales recognize wisdom when they see it, and the pod survives because the wise elders show the way. The rest of the whales can swim in the wake of their truth. Menopausal whales are surprisingly #Sexy.

We all need to surround young parents with the support they need to be wonderful, peaceful parents at the center of their children's lives

while working meaningfully, in a co-creative way. The leaders aren't who we thought they were. But they are emerging now, and the old systems that feel so painful will change—or die. Not a moment too soon.

*

"Come mothers and fathers throughout the land
And don't criticize what you can't understand
Your sons and your daughters are beyond your command
Your old road is rapidly agin'
Please get out of the new one if you can't lend your hand
For the times they are a' changin'!"
—Bob Dylan, "The Times They Are a Changin'," 1964

The Math of Empathy: What and How We Count Matters

Math is the most universal of languages and, some would say, it's like postcards from the grand designer of it all. Take pi, for instance. *Come on!* 3.14159 etc.

The math of the grand design is mind-blowing, especially as you look out into the universe or deeper and deeper into the way our world is organized. Crystals. DNA. The periodic table. Sometimes we get confused and think this is all our doing. It's not. We didn't invent any of it, but we can marvel at and learn from the order of it all.

The math we invented was much simpler. We first started counting around the time of the agricultural revolution. Addition. Subtraction. Accounting. Simple stuff, but a big shift, nonetheless. Instead of existing in a fog together, we became specialized and started valuing certain things and jobs and time more than others. Doing so separated us more than it brought us together, but since empathy is selfish first, it was a necessary step.

What's the math of the industrial revolution? How many widgets can 30 people make if lined up production-style for 10 hours a day? Products. Of. Multiplication. Productivity speeding up. More things with fewer people. More stuff in less time. We call that efficiency, but human connectivity and empathy took a back seat. Now, the possibility of abundance sets the table for cooperation at a grander scale. The technological revolution brought us to exponential math. Moore's law.

Faster, and faster, but still linear, entropic growth. Greater possibilities for physical abundance and global connectivity, setting the table for including emotional variables.

So, what's next? What happens when the math of entropy gives way to the math of empathy? Remember fractals? Growing infinitely from the inside out? Maybe we've been incomplete in our view of math until now. We've been optimizing physical resources, but the function we should be optimizing is time spent increasing the only resource on earth that is infinite—empathy. Maybe we should take some clues from nature and find this kind of resonance in our civilization as well. Fractals are networked. Fractals are inclusive. Fractals grow from the inside out. We can't know for sure, but maybe there is something about fractals we should be paying more attention to now. Something more divine than any human design. In any case, there are many fractals in nature, and aren't they beautiful?!

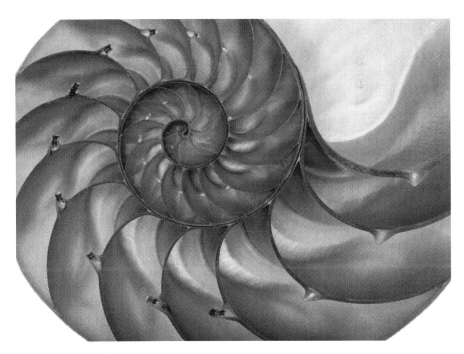

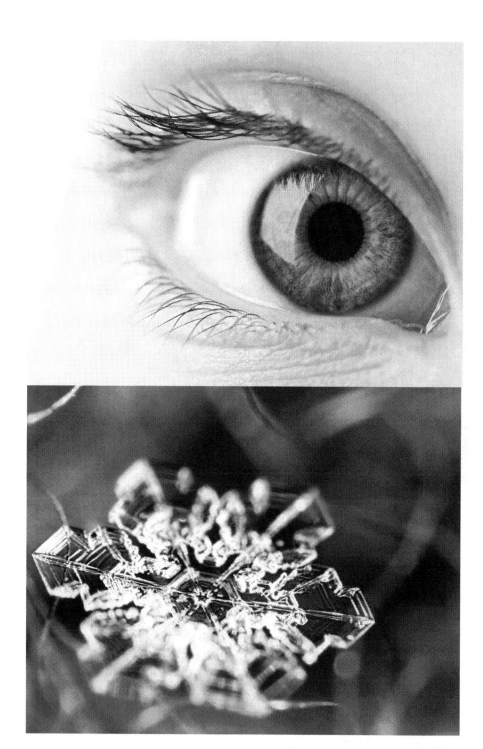

Evolutionary Changes in Real Time: Epigenetics of Empathy

"DNA is not just a sequence of letters; it's not just a script.
DNA is a dynamic movie. Our experiences are being
written into this movie, which is interactive."
—Moshe Szyf, Epigeneticist, TEDxBratislava, July 2016

If evolution feels like a soft science, over time frames too large to fathom, epigenetics is a relief. This growing field is providing us with the opportunity to witness the deep and lasting power of affective empathy as it unfolds. Epigenetics is the study of how our environment and relationships affect our DNA in real time. Our DNA is both ancient and dynamic, and chemical changes in DNA in reaction to environment underlie evolution.

In the labs of Michael Meaney and Moshe Szyf, scientists are studying how the impact of parenting in the earliest days changes the brain structures and DNA of children. They've watched rat babies, monkeys (our cousins) and their babies; they've even watched human children, for whom the environmental experiment is underway in the real world rather than simulated in a lab.

Here's what they've found: Rat babies who are licked by their mothers and monkeys who are raised by moms rather than nurse monkeys grow into more secure, less stressed, less addiction-prone adults.[175] Their early experiences prepare their bodies for an abundant world, about which they can be endlessly curious, rather than a scarce world that requires fight or flight. This early orientation shows up in their behavior, and it shows up in the methylation patterns of their DNA. It's not soft at all; it becomes hardwired. Similarly, human babies grow up differently depending on the level of stress to them and their parents as well, manifesting similarly in their DNA.

So it goes with our capacity for empathy. Research has shown that early experiences have the power to change neural networks associated with empathic capacity, DNA, and behaviors in children. Neuroplasticity gives us the chance to keep changing and evolving, hopefully toward greater curiosity and abundance and empathy; but of course, that continues to depend on environment and experience.

Women Have
More Empathy
Than Men...So Far

Research suggests that women have more empathy than men. Women pick up yawns about 55% of the time, whereas men only do so 40% of the time.[176]

Women also identify more readily with other people's emotions. In a multitude of self-report questionnaires, women's responses consistently reflect more empathy than men. The same goes for studies using more objective measures such as functional MRI (fMRI).[177] In a 2006 article in the journal *Nature*, both sexes show activation of empathy in response to another's pain as indicated by blood flow in the fronto-insular and anterior cingulate cortices. However, in men but not in women, blood flow to these areas decreased when the person receiving the pain was perceived as unfair.[178] Men were able to escape the pain through perception or cognition, perhaps a narrative like, "He's getting what he deserved."

Mirror neuron research also suggests that women have more empathy than men. Mirror neurons are brain cells foundational to empathy. Neurophysiologists at the University of Parma identified "mirror neurons" in the inferior frontal cortex and anterior parietal lobe of our brains. Mirror neurons are so named because they fire when primates act and observe the same action performed by another.[179]

When it comes to mirror neurons, women have more. By using fMRI, transcranial magnetic stimulation (TMS), electroencephalography (EEG), magnetoencephalography (MEG), and event-related brain potential (ERP), several studies have shown that women report greater activity in neural networks associated with mirroring systems.[180]

Of course, there are great differences within gender, as well. You probably know some empathically gifted men as well as women who can't pick up on social cues at all. But overall, women leaders have more empathic capacity and little girls have more mirror neurons.

The question is...*why?* Because women have the home-field advantage.

"We are what we repeatedly do."
—Aristotle

Some people believe that women are biologically wired to be empathic while men are wired to be competitive. While biology certainly plays a role, we know that environment also influences who we are. So it makes sense to ask: Are there experiences that build women's capacity for empathy? Is there something that women *do* that makes them catch yawns more easily than men? Is it possible that what women really have is a "home-field advantage"?

The most obvious experience that comes to mind is the hands-on caring that women do, particularly in raising children.

Our physiology explains how we first got the home-field advantage. Women were the ones who gave birth, so they were automatically in the room, hormonally primed and ready at the go with food from their breasts. It made sense that they would do the caring that ensued. It made sense that women would be the ones to partake in the life-giving dance of affective empathy. But just as this dance has a profound impact on the baby, it also has a profound effect on the mother.

Notes

Chapter 1

1 http://news.gallup.com/poll/180404/gallup-daily-employee-engagement.aspx

2 https://www.washingtonpost.com/news/to-your-health/wp/2017/06/30/the-u-s-fertility-rate-just-hit-a-historic-low-why-some-demographers-are-freaking-out/ See also https://www.nytimes.com/2018/02/13/upshot/american-fertility-is-falling-short-of-what-women-want.html

Chapter 2

3 https://en.wikipedia.org/wiki/Robert_Vischer

4 Frans de Waal, *The Age of Empathy: Nature's Lessons for a Kinder Society* (New York: Broadway Books, 2010), 68.

5 De Waal, *Empathy,* 208–209.

6 For a full explanation of the state of science and the empathy circuit, check out Simon Baron-Cohen, *The Science of Evil: On Empathy and the Origins of Cruelty* (New York: Basic Books, 2012), 17–43.

7 De Waal, *Empathy,* 204-205.

8 Ibid.

9 http://www.wsj.com/articles/SB110989327130070064

10 http://bostonreview.net/forum/against-empathy/simon-baron-cohen-response-against-empathy-baron-cohen

11 Ibid.

12 https://www.nytimes.com/roomfordebate/2016/12/29/does-empathy-guide-or-hinder-moral-action

13   Jeremy Rifkin, *The Empathic Civilization: The Race to Global Consciousness in a World of Crisis* (New York: Tarcher Perigree, 2009), 2.

14   Cheikh Anta Diop, *The African Origin of Civilization: Myth or Reality* ed. Mercer Cook (Chicago: Chicago Review Press, 1989)

15   Peter H. Diamandis and Steven Kotler, *Abundance: The Future is Better Than You Think* (New York: Simon & Schuster, 2012)

16   Yuval Noah Harari, *Sapiens: A Brief History of Humankind* (New York: Harper, 2015), 366–367.

17   Rifkin, *Empathic Civilization,* 171.

Chapter 3

18   https://www.thebalance.com/leadership-definition-2948275

19   https://en.oxforddictionaries.com/definition/us/compensation

20   https://en.wikipedia.org/wiki/Mansplaining

21   Rebecca Solnit, *Men Explain Things to Me* (Chicago: Haymarket Books, 2014).

22   https://en.wikipedia.org/wiki/Gordon_Gekko

23   De Waal, *Age of Empathy,* 63.

24   Paul Babiak, Craig S. Neumann and Robert D. Hare, "Corporate Psychopathy: Talking the Walk," *Behavioral Sciences & the Law* 28, no. 2 (2010): 174-193, https://doi.org/10.1002/bsl.925.

25   https://www.psychology.org.au/news/media_releases/13September2016/Brooks

26   Diana Henriques, "New Description of Timing on Madoff's Confession," *The New York Times,* January 13, 2009. Retrieved January 19, 2009.

27   https://www.sec.gov/litigation/litreleases/lr17001.htm

28   http://fortune.com/2016/07/21/roger-ailes-resigned-scandal-timeline

29   https://www.forbes.com/sites/emilywillingham/2016/08/23/ceo-of-mylan-pharmaceuticals-sees-671-salary-increase-in-8-years/#15ab6e8f1972

30   http://www.atlantamagazine.com/great-reads/no-accident-inside-gms-deadly-ignition-switch-scandal

31   https://www.popularmechanics.com/cars/a6700/top-automotive-engineering-failures-ford-pinto-fuel-tanks

32   https://www.nytimes.com/2018/03/19/technology/facebook-cambridge-analytica-explained.html

33   http://footwearnews.com/2018/business/executive-moves/nike-vice-president-jayme-martin-exits-misconduct-519441

34   http://www.moneycontrol.com/news/features/richard-fuld-life-after-lehman-crisis_950796.html?utm_source=ref_article

35   http://www.dannysearle.com/images/Book/Download/Corporate%20Psychopathy%20Talking%20the%20Walk%20-%20Paul%20Babiak,.pdf

36 https://historicalunderbelly.files.wordpress.com/2012/12/corporate-psychopaths.pdf

37 https://www.jstor.org/stable/40929370?seq=1#page_scan_tab_contents

38 https://www.businesstrainingworks.com/onsite-training-fees

Chapter 4

39 http://news.gallup.com/poll/181289/majority-employees-not-engaged-despite-gains-2014.aspx

40 https://www.bankrate.com/personal-finance/smart-money/economic-survey-may-2018/

41 http://www.gallup.com/poll/181289/majority-employees-not-engaged-despite-gains-2014.aspx

42 Quoted by Robert F. Bruner, http://faculty.darden.virginia.edu/brunerb/Bruner_PDF/Does%20M&A%20Pay.pdf

43 http://www.wsj.com/articles/the-economys-hidden-problem-were-out-of-big-ideas-1481042066

44 http://downloads.realviewtechnologies.com/Technology%20Review/Technology%20Review/November%20December%202012.pdf

45 MCK,"Was That It?" *The Economist,* September 8, 2012.

46 Dane Stangler, *High Growth Firms and the Future of the American Economy* (Kansas City, MO: Ewing Marion Kauffman Foundation, March 2010).

47 Statistics come from Christensen and Raynor, *The Innovator's Solution* (Boston: Harvard Business Review, 2003).

48 Holly Wood, "The Delusions of 'Heroic' Innovation," https://medium.com/@girlziplocked/the-delusions-of-heroic-innovation-e6857b256ec6

49 Matt Ruby, "'Side Hustle' as a Sign of the Apocalypse," https://medium.com/sandpapersuit/side-hustle-as-a-sign-of-the-apocalypse-e7027a889fc2

50 Ibid.

Chapter 5

51 Rifkin, *Empathic Civilization,* 537–8.

52 Paul Mason, *Postcapitalism: A Guide to Our Future* (New York: Farrar, Straus and Giroux, 2015), 119.

53 Jeremy Rifkin, *The Zero Marginal Cost Society: The Internet of Things, the Collaborative Commons, and the Eclipse of Capitalism* (New York: St. Martin's Press, 2014), 1.

54 https://hbr.org/2014/11/from-the-knowledge-economy-to-the-human-economy

55 Joe Brewer, "The Pain You Feel is Capitalism Dying," https://medium.com/keep-learning-keep-growing/the-pain-you-feel-is-capitalism-dying-5cdbe06a936c

56 Mason, *Postcapitalism,* 126.

57 http://www.nytimes.com/2016/06/08/technology/online-searches-can-identify-cancer-victims-study-finds.html?smprod=nytcore-iphone&smid=nytcore-iphone-share

58 Joseph Jaworski, *Synchronicity: The Inner Path of Leadership* ed. Betty Sue Flowers (Oakland: Berrett-Koehler Publishers, 2011).

59 Thomas L. Freidman, *The World Is Flat: A Brief History of the Twenty-First Century* (New York: Farrar, Straus, and Giroux, 2006).

60 Rifkin, *Zero Marginal Cost Society,* 69.

61 Kevin Kelly, "New Rules for the New Economy," *Wired*, Sept. 1, 1997. https://www.wired.com/1997/09/newrules

62 Rifkin, *Empathic Civilization,* 532–33.

63 Yochai Benkler, *The Wealth of Networks: How Social Production Transforms Markets and Freedom* (New Haven, CT: Yale University Press, 2007).

64 https://www.nytimes.com/2017/01/04/opinion/from-hands-to-heads-to-hearts.html

65 Kelly, "New Rules for the New Economy."

66 Mason, *Postcapitalism,* 143.

67 Rifkin, *Empathic Civilization,* 532–533.

68 See note 64.

69 Rifkin, *Empathic Civilization,* 160.

Chapter 7

70 https://www.brookings.edu/wp-content/uploads/2016/06/08_innovation_greenstone_looney.pdf

71 http://learningenglish.voanews.com/a/eight-men-worth-as-much-as-half-global-population/3678656.html

72 Daron Acemoğlu and James A. Robinson, *Why Nations Fail: The Origins of Power, Prosperity, and Poverty* (New York: Crown Business, 2012)

73 See https://www.wsj.com/articles/companies-try-a-new-strategy-empathy-1466501403; primary research from https://hbr.org/2015/11/2015-empathy-index.

74 www.currencyofemapthy.com

Chapter 8

75 https://disneyworld.disney.go.com/fastpass-plus

76 Madeleine L'Engle, *Walking on Water: Reflections on Faith and Art* (New York: Convergent, 2016), p. 17.

77 Wendell Pierce, Speech at Chautauqua Institution, Chautauqua, NY, August 25, 2016.

78 John D. Mayer, Peter Salovey, and David Caruso, "Emotional Intelligence: Theory, Findings, and Implications," *Psychological Inquiry*, 15, no. 3 (2004): 197–215.

79 Daniel Goleman, *Emotional Intelligence: Why It Can Matter More Than IQ* (New York: Bantam, 1995).

Chapter 9

80   https://scholar.harvard.edu/files/goldin/files/goldin_aeapress_2014_1.pdf

81   De Waal, *Age of Empathy,* 67.

82   Sarah Blaffer Hrdy, *Mother Nature: Maternal Instincts and How They Shape the Human Species* (New York: Ballantine, 2000), 41–42.

83   James K. Riling and Larry Young, "The Biology of Mammalian Parenting and Its Effect on Offspring Social Development," *Science* 345, no. 6198 (August 2014): 771-776, https://doi.org/10.1126/science.1252723.

84   Ruth Feldman,"The Adaptive Human Parental Brain: Implications for Children's Social Development," *Trends in Neurosciences* 38, no. 6 (May 2015): https://doi.org/10.1016/j.tins.2015.04.004.

85   http://www.pnas.org/content/112/45/13805.abstract

86   https://www.ncbi.nlm.nih.gov/pubmed/26497119

Chapter 10

87   Arlie Hochschild, *Time Bind: When Work Becomes Home and Home Becomes Work* (New York: Holt, 2001).

88   http://www.pewsocialtrends.org/2014/04/08/after-decades-of-decline-a-rise-in-stay-at-home-mothers/

89   https://en.wikipedia.org/wiki/Cognitive_dissonance

90   Baron-Cohen, *Science of Evil,* 75.

91   https://www.npr.org/sections/health-shots/2016/10/17/497942331/npr-poll-are-parents-overrating-the-quality-of-child-care; https://www1.nichd.nih.gov/publications/pubs/documents/seccyd_06.pdf

92   http://www.cleveland.com/metro/index.ssf/2016/12/preschools_should_start_young_include_health_care_and_motherly_love_study_finds.html#incart_river_mobileshort_home

93   https://www.nytimes.com/2015/04/02/upshot/yes-your-time-as-a-parent-does-make-a-difference.html?rref=upshot

Chapter 11

94   Amy Chua, *Battle Hymn of the Tiger Mother* (New York: Penguin Press, 2011).

95   https://www.theatlantic.com/magazine/archive/2012/07/why-women-still-cant-have-it-all/309020/

96   http://www.pewresearch.org/fact-tank/2014/12/22/less-than-half-of-u-s-kids-today-live-in-a-traditional-family/

97   http://www.bentley.edu/impact/articles/nowuknow-why-millennials-refuse-get-married

98   See: https://www.nytimes.com/2018/02/13/upshot/american-fertility-is-falling-short-of-what-women-want.html; see also: https://www.technologyreview.com/s/603065/rejuvenating-the-chance-of-motherhood/

99   https://www.cdc.gov/nchs/nvss/vsrr/natality-dashboard.htm

100 Meghan Daum, ed., *Selfish, Shallow, and Self-Absorbed: Sixteen Writers on the Decision Not to Have Kids* (New York: Picador, 2015).

Chapter 12

101 http://money.cnn.com/2016/09/27/news/companies/sheryl-sandberg-women-workplace-study/?iid=EL

102 https://www.nytimes.com/interactive/2017/01/13/us/politics/trump-cabinet-women-minorities.html?_r=0

103 http://www.catalyst.org/knowledge/women-government

104 https://philanthropy.com/article/Lack-of-Women-in-Top-Roles/153197

105 Marc Goulden, Karie Frasch, Mary Ann Mason, and The Center for American Progress, *Staying Competitive: Patching America's Leaky Pipeline in the Sciences* (2009): 2.

106 http://qz.com/818534/the-us-just-plummeted-down-the-world-economic-forum-rankings-for-gender-equality-in-work-and-politics/

107 https://www.weforum.org/reports/the-global-gender-gap-report-2016

108 See note 106.

109 http://www.mckinsey.com/business-functions/organization/our-insights/why-diversity-matters

110 http://www.ey.com/us/en/newsroom/news-releases/news-ey-new-research-from-the-peterson-institute-for-international-economics-and-ey-reveals-significant-correlation-between-women-in-corporate-leadership-and-profitability

Chapter 13

111 J. D. Vance, *Hillbilly Elegy: A Memoir of a Family and Culture in Crisis* (New York: Harper, 2016).

112 See p. 4 of: http://georgemaciunas.com/wp-content/uploads/2012/06/Economic-Possibilities-of-Our-Grandchildren.pdf

113 https://www.youtube.com/watch?v=8NPzLBSBzPI

114 https://mic.com/articles/167417/maximum-number-of-hours-you-should-work-each-week-to-be-healthy-according-to-research?bt_ee=i3lykgiE446c6oxR9lVWIW/xHvlZT0prJ4boU4X1jz9ALYd8sA7dPHeO/bjEfieY&bt_ts=1486091440363#.AR5IVNt50

115 http://www.cnbc.com/2017/01/03/why-finland-is-ahead-of-the-us-with-guaranteed-income.html

Chapter 14

116 https://theconversation.com/dads-are-more-involved-in-parenting-yes-but-moms-still-put-in-more-work-72026; see also https://theconversation.com/fathers-also-want-to-have-it-all-study-says-60910

117 http://www.caregiving.org/wp-content/uploads/2015/05/2015_CaregivingintheUS_Final-Report-June-4_WEB.pdf. See also: Guilia M. Dotti Sani and Judith Treas, "Educational Gradients in Parents' Child-Care Time Across Countries, 1965-2012," *Journal of Marriage and Family* 78, no. 4 (August 2016): 1083-1096, https://doi.org/10.1111/jomf.12305.

118 Sarah Blaffer Hrdy, *Mother Nature,* 174.

119 Ibid., 100 (italics ours).

120 Katherine Ellison, *The Mommy Brain: How Motherhood Makes Us Smarter* (New York: Basic Books, 2006), 150.

121 Ibid.

122 Ibid., 152.

Chapter 15

123 De Waal, *Age of Empathy,* 220.

124 Lisa K. Richardson, B. Christopher Fruehm and Ronald Acierno, "Prevalence Estimates of Combat-Related Post-Traumatic Stress Disorder: Critical Review," *Australian & New Zealand Journal of Psychiatry* 44, no. 1 (January 2010): 4-19, https://doi.org/10.3109/00048670903393597.

125 https://www.goodtherapy.org/blog/military-resiliency-training

126 De Waal, *Age of Empathy,* 194.

127 https://ucr.fbi.gov/crime-in-the-u.s/2015/crime-in-the-u.s.-2015/tables/table-66

128 Bridget F. Grant et al., "Prevalence, Correlates, Disability, and Comorbidity of DSM-IV Borderline Personality Disorder: Results from the Wave 2 National Epidemiologic Survey on Alcohol and Related Conditions," *The Journal of Clinical Psychiatry* 69, no. 4 (2008): 533–545, https://www.ncbi.nlm.nih.gov/pmc/articles/PMC2676679/. See also: Frederick S. Stinson et al., "Prevalence, Correlates, Disability, and Comorbidity of DSM-IV Narcissistic Personality Disorder: Results From the Wave 2 National Epidemiologic Survey on Alcohol and Related Conditions," *The Journal of Clinical Psychiatry* 69, no. 7 (2008): 1033-1045, https://doi.org/10.4088/JCP.v69n0701.

129 Statistics from: American Psychiatric Association, *Diagnostic and Statistical Manual of Mental Disorders: DSM-IV-TR.* (Washington, DC: American Psychiatric Association, 2000); see also: Leonardo Christov-Moore et al., "Empathy: Gender Effects in Brain and Behavior," *Neuroscience and Biobehavioral Reviews* 46, pt. 4 (2014): 604–627, https://doi.org/10.1016/j.neubiorev.2014.09.001.

Chapter 16

130 https://www.nytimes.com/2017/01/04/upshot/why-men-dont-want-the-jobs-done-mostly-by-women.html

Chapter 17

131 https://www.brookings.edu/wp-content/uploads/2017/08/casetextsp17bpea.pdf

132 https://johnwayne.com/quotes/

133 Ellison, *Mommy Brain,* 151.

Chapter 18

134 Dotti Sani and Treas, "Educational Gradients in Parents' Child-Care Time Across Countries."

135 Erna Furman, *Toddlers and Their Mothers: A Study in Early Personality Development* (Madison, CT: International Universities Press, 1992).

136 Nancy Chodorow, *The Reproduction of Mothering: Psychoanalysis and the Sociology of Gender* (Berkeley: University of California Press, 1999).

137 Ibid.

138 To hear Fred Rogers' testimony, see: https://www.youtube.com/watch?v=fKy7ljRr0AA.

139 http://www.neighborhoodarchive.com/music/songs/what_do_you_do.html

Chapter 19

140 https://www.facebook.com/events/731328973612433/

141 Andrew Solomon, *Far from the Tree: Parents, Children and the Search for Identity* (New York: Scribner, 2012).

142 https://www.npr.org/sections/ed/2016/07/01/484325664/babies-of-color-are-now-the-majority-census-says

143 https://en.wikipedia.org/wiki/Daryl_Davis

144 https://opinionator.blogs.nytimes.com/2015/10/15/a-feminism-where-leaning-in-means-leaning-on-others/?_r=0

Chapter 20

145 https://apnews.com/9079eca84bc542a7bdd79b65fae1e53f/Americans-pessimistic-about-Trump,-country:-AP-NORC-Poll

146 https://fivethirtyeight.com/features/americans-distaste-for-both-trump-and-clinton-is-record-breaking/

147 https://www.merriam-webster.com/dictionary/swoon

148 https://www.washingtonpost.com/politics/i-learned-because-of-fred-trump-cites-brothers-struggle-in-talking-about-addiction/2017/10/26/36644da4-ba84-11e7-be94-fabb0f1e9ffb_story

149 http://www.gallup.com/poll/202742/obama-averages-job-approval-president.aspx

150 https://www.cnn.com/2017/02/27/politics/george-w-bush-paintings/index.html

151 https://www.flickr.com/photos/ninian_reid/28410733620

152 Frans de Waal, *Chimpanzee Politics: Power and Sex among Apes*, 25th anniversary ed. (Baltimore: Johns Hopkins University Press, 2007).

Chapter 21

153 "It Takes Two" was written and recorded in 1965 by Marvin Gaye and Kim Weston; the song was covered and made popular by Sonny and Cher in the 1970s.

154 https://upload.wikimedia.org/wikipedia/commons/9/9d/Komodo_dragon_with_tongue.jpg

155 http://www.findingdulcinea.com/features/science/environment/Parthenogenesis--When-Animals-Reproduce-Without-a-Mate.html

156 https://www.newscientist.com/article/2107219-exclusive-worlds-first-baby-born-with-new-3-parent-technique/

157 http://leb.net/gibran/

158 Rilling and Young, "The Biology of Mammalian Parenting and Its Effect on Offspring Social Development."

159 Ellison, *Mommy Brain,* 150.

160 De Waal, *Age of Empathy,* 108.

161 Rifkin, *Empathic Civilization,* 173.

Chapter 23

162 Atsunori Ariga and Alejandro Lleras, "Brief and Rare Mental 'Breaks' Keep You Focused: Deactivation and Reactivation of Task Goals Preempt Vigilance Decrements," *Cognition* 118, no. 3 (2011): 439-443, https://doi.org/10.1016/j.cognition.2010.12.007.

Chapter 24

163 L'Engle, *Walking on Water.*

164 https://about.americanexpress.com/sites/americanexpress.newshq.businesswire.com/files/doc_library/file/2017_SWOB_Report_-FINAL.pdf

165 http://www.theatlantic.com/business/archive/2016/07/the-myth-of-the-millennial-entrepreneur/490058/

Chapter 25

166 http://www.forbes.com/sites/kathryndill/2014/04/15/report-ceos-earn-331-times-as-much-as-average-workers-774-times-as-much-as-minimum-wage-earners/#693f28fd78ef

167 Josh Harkinson, "America's 100 Richest People Control More Wealth than the Entire Black Population," *Mother Jones,* Dec. 2, 2015, https://www.motherjones.com/politics/2015/12/report-100-people-more-wealth-african-american-population/

168 Harari, *Sapiens,* 26–27.

169 https://blog.protegra.com/2014/07/07/startups-and-the-myth-of-sisyphus/

Chapter 26

170 Baron-Cohen, *Science of Evil.*

171 https://faculty.chicagobooth.edu/eob/edobrien_empathyPSPR.pdf

172 https://www.brookings.edu/research/how-millennials-could-upend-wall-street-and-corporate-america/

173 http://www.nytimes.com/2014/08/17/fashion/the-millennials-are-generation-nice.html

174 http://business.financialpost.com/executive/careers/is-the-me-generation-less-empathetic

Appendix B

175 Ian C. G. Weaver et al., "Epigenetic Programming by Maternal Behavior," *Nature Neuroscience* 7 (2004): 847-854, https://doi.org/10.1038/nn1276.

Appendix C

176 http://rsos.royalsocietypublishing.org/content/3/2/150459

177 Leonardo Christov-Moore et al., "Empathy: Gender Effects in Brain and Behavior," *Neuroscience & Biobehavioral Reviews* 46, pt. 4 (October 2014): 604-627, https://doi.org/10.1016/j.neubiorev.2014.09.001.

178 Tania Singer et al., "Empathic Neural Responses are Modulated by the Perceived Fairness of Others," *Nature* 439 (January 2006): 466-469, https://doi.org/10.1038/nature04271.

179 http://www.apa.org/monitor/oct05/mirror.aspx

180 See: Yawei Cheng et al., "Gender Differences In the Mu Rhythm of the Human Mirror-Neuron System," *PLoS One* 3, no. 5 (October 2018): e2113, https://doi.org/10.1371/journal.pone.0002113; Yawei Cheng et al., "The Perception of Pain In Others Suppresses Somatosensory Oscillations: a Magneto-encephalography Study," *NeuroImage* 40, no. 4 (May 2008): 1833–1840, https://doi.org/10.1016/j.neuroimage.2008.01.064; Yawei Cheng et al., "Sex Differences In the Neuroanatomy of Human Mirror-Neuron System: a Voxel-Based Morphometric Investigation," *Neuroscience* 158, no. 2 (January 2009): 713-720, https://doi.org/10.1016/j.neuroscience.2008.10.026; Chia-Yen Yang et al., "Gender Differences In the Mu Rhythm During Empathy for Pain: An Electroencephalographic Study," *Brain Research* 1251, (January 2009): 176-184, https://doi.org/10.1016/j.brainres.2008.11.062; and see Martin Schulte-Rüther et al., "Gender Differences In Brain Networks Supporting Empathy," *NeuroImage* 42, no. 1 (August 2008): 393–403, https://doi.org/10.1016/j.neuroimage.2008.04.180.

Selected Bibliography

Acho, Jaqueline, Eva Basilion, and Monica Tanase-Coles. Organizational Diagnostic: Currency of Empathy®. www.currencyofemapthy.com.

American Psychiatric Association, *Diagnostic and Statistical Manual of Mental Disorders: DSM-IV-TR.* Washington, DC: American Psychiatric Association, 2000.

Ariga, Atsunori and Alejandro Lleras. "Brief and Rare Mental 'Breaks' Keep You Focused: Deactivation and Reactivation of Task Goals Preempt Vigilance Decrements," *Cognition* 118, no. 3 (2011): 439-443, https://doi.org/10.1016/j.cognition.2010.12.007.

Baron-Cohen, Simon. *The Science of Evil: On Empathy and the Origins of Cruelty.* New York: Basic Books, 2010.

Benkler, Yochai. *The Wealth of Networks: How Social Production Transforms Markets and Freedom.* New Haven, CT: Yale University Press, 2007.

Cheng, Yawei, Kun Hsien Chou, Jean Decety, I. Yun Chen, Daisy Liang Hung, Ovid Jyh Lang Tzeng, and Ching Po Lin. "Sex Differences In the Neuroanatomy of Human Mirror-Neuron System: a Voxel-Based Morphometric Investigation," *Neuroscience* 158, no. 2, (January 2009): 713–720.

Cheng, Yawei, Po-Lei Lee, Chia-Yen Yang, Ching-Po Lin, Daisy Hung, and Jean Decety . "Gender Differences In the Mu Rhythm of the Human Mirror-Neuron System," *PLoS One* 3, no. 5 (October 2018): e2113.

Cheng, Yawei, Chia-Yen Yang, Ching-Po Lin, Po-Lei Lee, and Jean Decety. "The Perception of Pain In Others Suppresses Somatosensory Oscillations: a Magneto-encephalography Study," *NeuroImage* 40, no. 4 (May 2008): 1833–1840.

Chodorow, Nancy. *Reproduction of Mothering: Psychoanalysis and the Sociology of Gender.* Berkeley: University of California Press, 1999.

Christensen, Clayton and Michael Raynor. *The Innovator's Solution.* Boston: Harvard Business Review, 2003.

de Waal, Frans. *The Age of Empathy: Nature's Lessons for a Kinder Society*. New York: Broadway Books, 2010.

Ellison, Katherine. *The Mommy Brain: How Motherhood Makes Us Smarter*. New York: Basic Books, 2006.

Friedman, Thomas. "From Hands to Heads to Hearts." *New York Times*, January 4, 2017. https://www.nytimes.com/2017/01/04/opinion/from-hands-to-heads-to-hearts.html.

Furman, Erna. *Toddlers and Their Mothers: A Study in Early Personality Development*. Madison, CT: International Universities Press, 1992.

Goleman, Daniel. *Emotional Intelligence: Why It Can Matter More Than IQ*. New York: Bantam, 1995.

Goulden, Mark, Karie Frasch, and Mary Ann Mason. *Staying Competitive: Patching America's Leaky Pipeline In the Sciences*. Washington, DC: Center for American Progress, 2009, 2.

Grant, Bridget F., S. Patricia Chou, Risë B. Goldstein, Boji Huang, Frederick S. Stinson, Tulshi D. Saha, Sharon M. Smith, Deborah A. Dawson, Attila J. Pulay, Roger P. Pickering, and W. June Ruan. "Prevalence, Correlates, Disability, and Comorbidity of DSM-IV Borderline Personality Disorder: Results from the Wave 2 National Epidemiologic Survey on Alcohol and Related Conditions," *The Journal of Clinical Psychiatry* 69, no. 4 (2008): 533–545. https://www.ncbi.nlm.nih.gov/pmc/articles/PMC2676679/.

Harari, Yuval Noah. *Sapiens: A Brief History of Humankind*. New York: Harper, 2015.

Harkinson, Josh. "America's 100 Richest People Control More Wealth than the Entire Black Population." *Mother Jones*, December 2, 2015. https://www.motherjones.com/politics/2015/12/report-100-people-more-wealth-african-american-population/.

Henriques, Diana. "New Description of Timing on Madoff's Confession." *New York Times*, January 13, 2009.

Hochschild, Arlie. *Time Bind: When Work Becomes Home and Home Becomes Work*. New York: Holt, 2001.

Hrdy, Sarah Blaffer. *Mother Nature: Maternal Instincts and How They Shape the Human Species*. New York: Ballantine, 2000.

Kelly, Kevin. "New Rules for the New Economy." *Wired*, Sept. 1, 1997. https://www.wired.com/1997/09/newrules.

L'Engle, Madeleine. *Walking on Water: Reflections on Faith and Art*. New York: Convergent, 2016.

Mason, Paul. *Postcapitalism: A Guide to Our Future*. New York: Farrar, Straus and Giroux, 2015.

Mayer, John D., Peter Salovey, and David Caruso. "Emotional Intelligence: Theory, Findings, and Implications." *Psychological Inquiry, Inquiry* 15, no. 3 (2004), 197–215.

Pierce, Wendell. Speech at Chautauqua Institution. Chautauqua, NY, August 25, 2016

Richardson, Lisa K., B. Christopher Fruehm and Ronald Acierno, "Prevalence Estimates of Combat-Related Post-Traumatic Stress Disorder: Critical Review," *Australian & New Zealand Journal of Psychiatry* 44, no. 1 (January 2010): 4-19. https://doi.org/10.3109/00048670903393597.

Rifkin, Jeremy. *The Empathic Civilization: The Race to Global Consciousness in a World of Crisis.* New York: Tarcher Perigree, 2009.

Rifkin, Jeremy. *The Zero Marginal Cost Society: The Internet of Things, the Collaborative Commons, and the Eclipse of Capitalism.* New York: St. Martin's Press, 2014.

Riling, James K. and Larry Young, "The Biology of Mammalian Parenting and Its Effect on Offspring Social Development," *Science* 345, no. 6198 (August 2014): 771-776. https://doi.org/10.1126/science.1252723.

Rogers, Fred. Testimony Before US Congress, Washington, DC, May 1, 1969. https://www.youtube.com/watch?v=fKy7ljRr0AA.

Schulte-Rüther, Martin, Hans J. Markowitsch, N. Jon Shah, Gereon R. Fink, and Martina Piefke. "Gender Differences In Brain Networks Supporting Empathy," *NeuroImage* 42, no. 1 (August 2008): 393–403. https://doi.org/10.1016/j.neuroimage.2008.04.180.

Singer, Tania, Ben Seymour, John P. O'Doherty, Klaas E. Stephan, Raymond J. Dolan, and Chris D. Frith. "Empathic Neural Responses are Modulated by the Perceived Fairness of Others," *Nature* 439 (January 2006): 466-469. https://doi.org/10.1038/nature04271.

Solomon, Andrew. *Far from the Tree: Parents, Children, and the Search for Identity.* New York: Scribner, 2012.

Stangler, Dane. *High Growth Firms and the Future of the American Economy.* Kansas City, MO: Ewing Marion Kauffman Foundation, March 2010.

Willaims, Ray. "Is the 'Me Generation' Less Empathetic?" *Financial Post*, June 13, 2010. https://business.financialpost.com/executive/careers/is-the-me-generation-less-empathetic.

Yang, Chia-Yen, Jean Decety, Shinyi Lee, Chenyi Chen, and Yawei Cheng. "Gender Differences In the Mu Rhythm During Empathy for Pain: An Electroencephalographic Study," *Brain Research* 1251, (January 2009): 176-184. https://doi.org/10.1016/j.brainres.2008.11.062.

Zaki, Jamil. "Does Empathy Guide or Hinder Moral Action?" Room for Debate, *New York Times*, December 29, 2016. https://www.nytimes.com/roomfordebate/2016/12/29/does-empathy-guide-or-hinder-moral-action.

Index

Acknowledgments

Grateful to live in loving relationships. We appreciate our parents, Peter and Barbara Acho and the late Costas and Kanella Vasiliades and extended family, especially Lia and Chris Barris, whose encouragement and conversations contributed greatly to this book. We can't imagine life without our #Sexy husbands, Jim Basilion and John LeMay, and their co-creative partnership, especially as parents to our kids. Our children, Kanella, Sophie, Grant, and Mary, are our most important teachers in so many ways.

We're so glad to understand that, thanks in no small part to the Hanna Perkins Center for Child Development in Cleveland, Ohio, where our partnership began and the seeds for this book were planted. We're still learning. We are especially grateful to Kay MacKenzie, Marilyn Salem, Judith Pitlick, Rique Sollish, Barbara Streeter, and Fatemah Toossi for their guidance and being there to bear witness.

Grateful to live in a place where empathy flows. Shaker Heights/Cleveland, Ohio, is special, filled with curious and thoughtful people who know inclusion is the only way and are willing and able to take risks as intrapreneurs and entrepreneurs. Throughout the writing of this book, their stories inspired us. They are making our community and the world a better place.

We appreciate hearing from them, including: Barbara Anderson, Donita Anderson, Jim Basilion, Kate Blaszak, Gwen Garth, Anthoula Gianniotis, Christopher Gibbons, Sue Gifford, Michael and Stacy Goldberg, Abra Goldman, Lynn-Ann Gries, Jane EsselsStyn and Brian Hart, Shelby Hersh, Sharon Sobol Jordan, Maxie C. Jackson III, Stewart Kohl, John LeMay, D. Scott Looney, Grant Marquit, Randall McShepherd, Amy Morgenstern, Veranda Rodgers, Joe Romano, Akua Saunders, Stephanie Silverman, Ann Smith, Angela and Nate Thompson, Marni Task, Jan Thrope, Lisa Weitzman, Andrew Wheaton, and Betty Worley. Deeply thoughtful and kind people provided early input on the manuscript: Jim Basilion, Christopher Gibbons, Robin Green, Brian Hart, Meg von der Heydt, Trevor Jones and John LeMay. They helped us move the conversation out into the world. From there, editor Elizabeth Brown took over and helped our baby become a book. She was our doula and we are so lucky to have found her. Jeffrey Bauer of the design firm Giraffe, Inc., skillfully and artistically helped make this beautiful book a reality to hold and read. James Steinberg, illustrator extraordinaire, helped dress up our book and made cover art fun. We appreciate our rock star proofreader Liberty Britz for her diligent work, Millennial perspectives, and encouragement. Thanks to Sandi Schroeder for indexing the book.

Grateful to live at this time, in which the potential for empathic consciousness is unbounded. It's not a given, but the network is alive, and fellowship is everywhere. The network's biggest gift to us was Monica Tanase-Coles, co-author of our Currency of Empathy® diagnostic, collaborator in client work, and life coach extraordinaire. Jen Lehner, fearless social media pioneer, helped us get started. The superpowers of affective empathy in Suzanne Borders, Kathryn Passov Edelman, and Karen Katz catalyzed and sustained us on many occasions. TEDxClevelandStateUniversity was the fire we needed to crystallize a story, thanks to Colette Hart and Nate Ward. Several other speaking invitations helped us continue to chip away at the marble and see what was really there, including: The Ashoka Future Forum, CEOs for Cities with Lee Fisher, The CFA Society of Cleveland, Accenture/KeyBank International Women's Day Celebration, Eaton Corporation with Harold Jones, Shaker Consulting with Brian Stern, Carnegie College, The Enspire Conference on Empathy in Education, Hartland & Co., and many more. Clients who have the courage to change systems are a constant source of inspiration, especially the Cleveland Division of Police. We appreciate the inspirational company of St. Paul's Episcopal Church in Cleveland Heights, Ohio, especially the Education for Ministry class of 2012, as well as the Jivasara satsang. We are grateful for Susan Koster and others who help us heal in a toxic world.

Finally, we are grateful to co-create. Great partnerships help us be brave. They really do. Writing, researching, and speaking together on these issues made the work so much better and way more fun than either of us could have had alone. We hope and pray that more people have chances to co-create in such a generative way. To make the world a better place...for all the children.

*

Authors

Jackie Acho is President of The Acho Group, a strategy and leadership consulting firm. Prior to founding her business in 2005, she was a partner of McKinsey & Company. For twenty-four years she has worked with clients on a variety of issues, with particular focus on innovation, strategy, and leadership development. Jackie and her colleagues write and speak about creating a Currency of Empathy®. In October 2014, she gave the TEDx talk: "A Good Day's Work Requires Empathy."

Jackie received her master's degree and PhD in inorganic chemistry from the Massachusetts Institute of Technology, and a BS in chemistry with highest honors from the University of Michigan in Ann Arbor. Jackie was named one of the "top 40 under 40" by Crain's *Cleveland Business* magazine, and "one of the 500 most influential women in Northeast Ohio" by *Northern Ohio Live* magazine.

Jackie has served on the Boards of Jumpstart, Inc., the National Inventors' Hall of Fame, the Urban League of Greater Cleveland, and the Research and Technology Commercialization Visiting Committee of Case Western Reserve University, among others. Jackie is a graduate of the Leadership Cleveland class of 2012. She taught "Finance in the Real World" at CWRU's Weatherhead School of Management and was a speaker in the Massively Open Online Course (MOOC) *Beyond Silicon Valley: Growing Entrepreneurship in Transitioning Economies.*

Jackie is a certified yoga teacher, Senior Warden of St. Paul's Episcopal Church in Cleveland Heights, and a graduate of Sewanee University's Education for Ministry program. She lives in Shaker Heights, Ohio, with her husband and children.

Learn more at www.currencyofempathy.com • www.jackieacho.com

Eva Basilion is a global health researcher, writer, and child advocate. She began her career at the International Trachoma Initiative, where her research established a new standard of treatment for the global elimination of blinding trachoma across 40 countries to treat over 80 million people.

After the birth of her second child, Eva became a stay-at-home mom. She co-founded Living Room Chat, a community support and education program for parents. She serves on the board of the Hanna Perkins Center for Child Development, whose mission is to foster the long-term emotional well-being of children using psychoanalytically informed theory and practice. She writes and blogs about the role of parenting in empathy, economics, and gender.

As the grown daughter of an early second-wave feminist who leaned out of the home with full force into her career, Eva brings a unique yet important perspective on the long-term implications of the early feminist movement on families and children. Her mission is to help complete the revolution in a way that benefits all. It's personal. Eva has a BA in economics from the University of Pennsylvania and an MS from the Harvard School of Public Health, where her studies with evolutionary biologist Richard Levins taught her that empathy is necessary and possible, even in science. Eva lives in Shaker Heights, Ohio, with her husband and two daughters.

A Note on Our Collaboration

We have been dear friends, as well as collaborators. We came to this work with a shared vision and a breadth and depth of experience. Our work styles are **very** different, but our love for each other and this work carried us through the rough spots. Between us, we...

Have one partner who never met a deadline she didn't hate
and another who has a hard time abiding when
people don't meet deadlines

Have one partner who explodes ideas onto a page then moves on,
and another who structures, restructures, and edits endlessly

Focus on content, poetry, logic, beauty, data,
the biggest thoughts and smallest details

Have four kids, ages 13 to 17

Spent a total of eight years learning about early childhood development
and helping our own babies, toddlers, and preschoolers grow at the renowned
Hanna Perkins School (HPS) in Shaker Heights, Ohio

Have grown up in cosmopolitan Washington, DC, and rust-belt Detroit,
and lived in Boston, Philadelphia, Chicago, and Spain

Have voted for Democrats, Republicans, and Independent candidates

Are first- and second-generation US citizens

Have family ethnicity that is Middle Eastern, Southern US, and Greek,
with backgrounds spanning the gamut of socioeconomic strata

Were raised by moms who worked full-throttle,
stayed home, and did something in between

Have leaned in full-throttle, stayed home with children,
and done something in between

Our friendship began over 12 years ago at the Hanna Perkins School in Shaker Heights, Ohio. As mothers of young children, we were both struggling to navigate the complicated terrain of early childhood. Through our experiences at HPS, we learned to forge stronger and more authentic connections with our children by learning to see the world through their eyes. In the process, we remembered things about ourselves we had long forgotten. We were never able to view the world in the same way again.

It was at morning drop-off that we started talking about the empathy we were learning through our children, contemplating how these concepts might apply to other areas of our lives, including work. We have been collaboratively writing and researching for the past decade, including the Currency of Empathy® blog and diagnostic in collaboration with our dear friend and colleague, Monica Tanase-Coles. Along the way, we have also helped each other take care of kids, recover from surgeries, face elder-parent care issues, bury a parent, and cook and eat great food; and we've enjoyed traveling together for business and pleasure.

We did not always agree, and it was not always easy! We came to recognize that the baby—the ART—emerged in the space between us. From our differing points of view, we shaped a new, more universal truth—something better than either of us could have created alone. In this way, we were not only students but living beneficiaries of a "currency of empathy."

*

www.empathydeficitdisorder.com